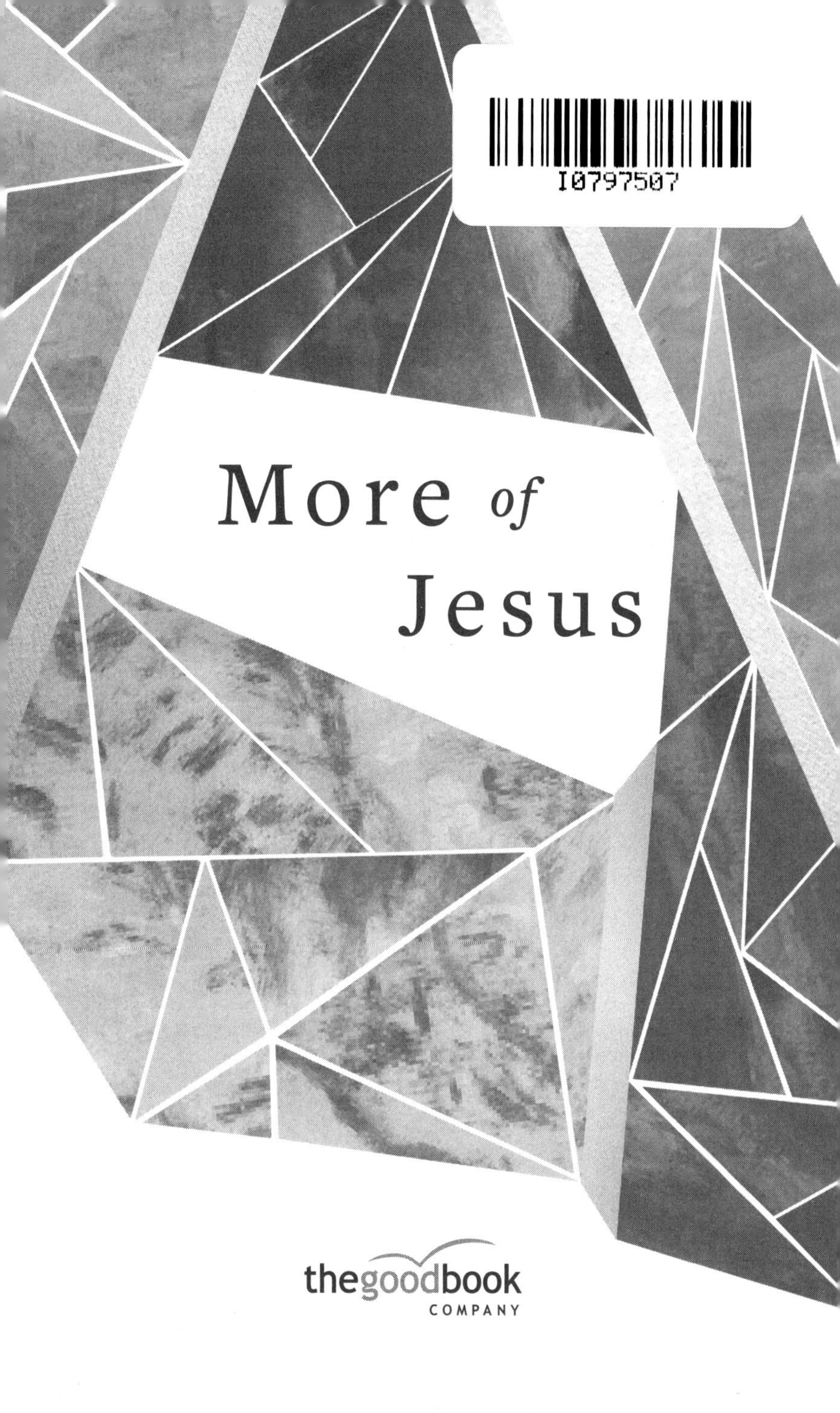
I0797507
More *of* Jesus
thegoodbook
COMPANY

More of Jesus

Published by:
The Good Book Company

thegoodbook.com | thegoodbook.co.uk
thegoodbook.com.au | thegoodbook.co.nz

Every book published by The Good Book Company has been written by a human author and edited by a human editor. While AI tools are sometimes used to assist with research and support certain processes, all content has been created by a human author and thoroughly checked by our editorial team to ensure it is biblically faithful and pastorally wise.

Cover design by Drew McCall.

ISBN: 9781802543704 | JOB-008437 | Printed in India

Contents

Introduction: An Invitation

The Lord Jesus is the greatest treasure in all the world, and knowing him will bring us the deepest joy. We will never exhaust his eternal excellencies. We will never have enough.

In 1838, William Gadsby wrote a hymn that beautifully captures the main conviction running through this book.

Immortal honours rest on Jesus' head,
My God, my portion and my living bread;
In him I live, upon him cast my care;
He saves from death, destruction and despair.

He is my refuge in each deep distress,
The Lord my strength and glorious righteousness;
Through floods and flames he leads me safely on
And daily makes his sovereign goodness known.

My every need he richly will supply,
Nor will his mercy ever let me die;
In him there dwells a treasure all divine,
And matchless grace has made that treasure mine.

O that my soul could love and praise him more,
His beauties trace, his majesty adore,
Live near his heart, rest in his love each day,
Hear his dear voice and all his will obey.

Whether you are just starting out on the journey or are many years down the road, this book is an invitation to come and discover more of Jesus.

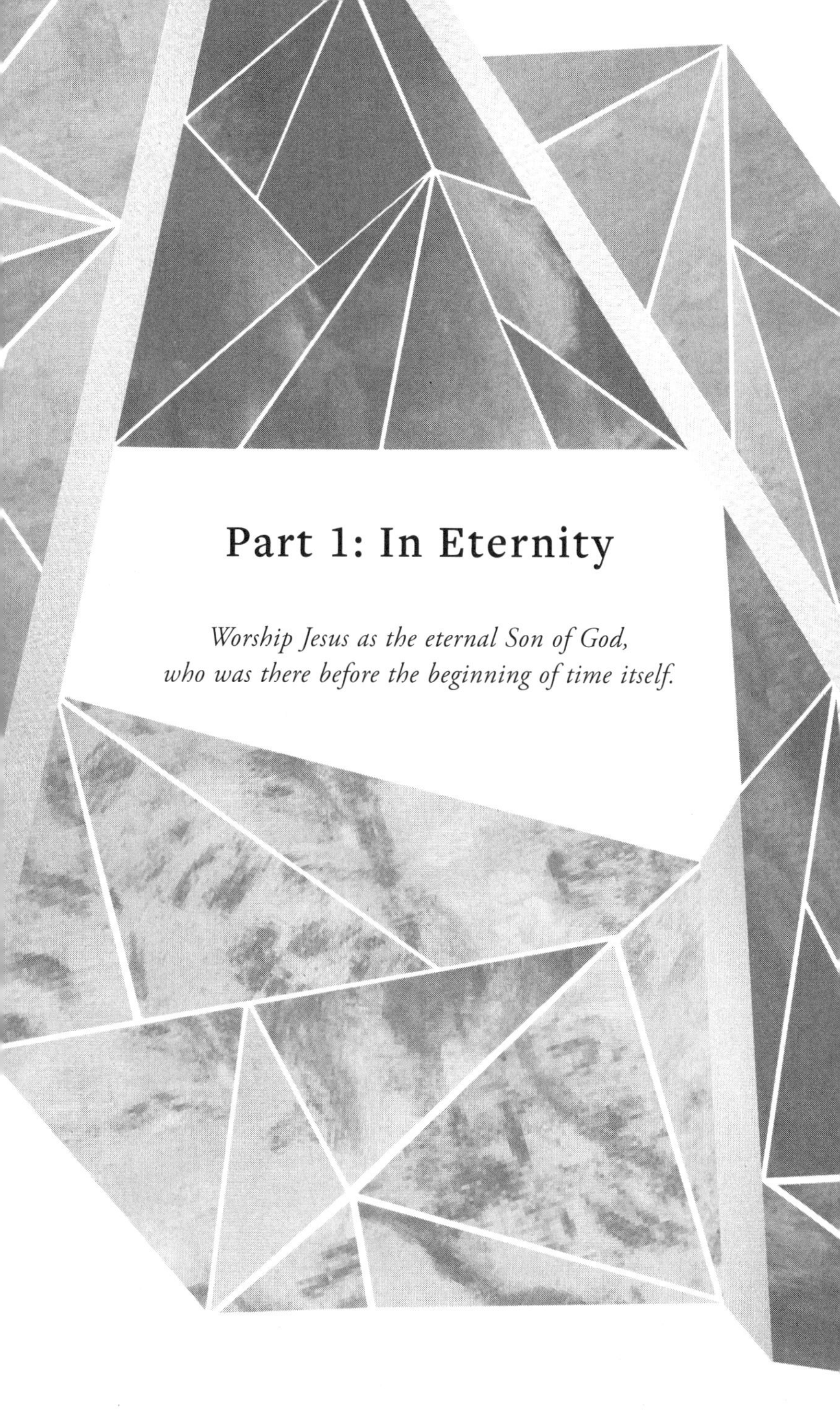

Part 1: In Eternity

Worship Jesus as the eternal Son of God,
who was there before the beginning of time itself.

The Word

In the beginning was the Word, and the Word was with God, and the Word was God. He was with God in the beginning.

John 1:1-2

What an opening sentence for a biography of Jesus! Human language is stretched to its absolute limit as the apostle John conveys truths of infinite complexity to our finite human minds.

Normally we learn by starting with the simple and building towards the difficult. Piano teachers begin with middle C and then slowly add in more notes. But not John. His approach is similar to a piano teacher who presents their eager little pupil with the magnificent glory of Tchaikovsky's Piano Concerto No. 1 (in B flat minor) at the first lesson. Many, many notes fill the page—far beyond the beginner's ability to comprehend or to play.

Of course, some might immediately slam the piano lid shut and never attempt to play again. But others will be captivated by the sheer wonder of the music in front of them. Something stirs within and a hunger to taste that glory for themselves motivates them to go back to middle C and start to learn.

Chapter 1 of John's Gospel is Tchaikovsky. It is not simplistic or basic—it isn't supposed to be. Rather it will leave us bewildered, excited, and hungry to understand what this sentence could possibly mean. John makes clear from the very start that Jesus is not just another man. He is the one who is worthy of a lifetime of meditation. Here is where we start our journey: out of our depth and yet stirred to taste glory itself.

Let's break it down a little. John talks about the "Word"—so far so good. We know about words and use them all the time. But then we find the first unsettling reality: this Word is a person (notice that "he" was with God in the beginning). And it's this person who is to become the whole subject of John's Gospel. God has a Word to give humanity, and his Word is Jesus.

John is only just getting started. He now tells us two truths about this Word that will take us back into eternity and deep into the very nature of God: he "was God" *and* "He was with God".

Do you feel the human language creaking under the weight of glory that is being expressed? How can you be *with* someone while at the same time *being* that person?

If John only wrote one of those things, there would be no problem. If we were just told that the Word was with God, we would simply assume that God created another being (called The Word) who existed alongside him. There is God and there is the Word. All cleared up and simple.

Or if John had only told us that the Word *was* God, again there would be no problem. We would simply assume that the Word is another name for God. There is no distinction between the Word and God because the Word is God. Right?

But John says both. The Word was with God (which implies distinctness between the Word and God) and also the Word was God (which implies oneness between the Word and God). That is what crunches our minds. In Jesus we meet the one who gives us a glimpse into the eternal God. Jesus has always been with God, and he has always been God. In a sentence of breathtaking genius, John captures the eternal glory that we are going to glimpse as we gaze at Jesus.

He is more than a figure of history. He is the God of eternity.

Let me spell this out... Before the manger and the donkey. Before the angel and the nativity. Before the baby was named Jesus. Before David, Moses and Abraham. Before the stars were flung into space and the earth was brought into being, the Word was there. He was with God. And he was God.

Jesus is wonderful because he is this Word. He is bigger than we can comprehend. He is greater than we could ever fathom. He is more worthy of worship than we could ever dream.

Do you find your heart stirred to get to know him more?

The Son

Jesus gave them this answer: "Very truly I tell you, the Son can do nothing by himself; he can do only what he sees his Father doing, because whatever the Father does the Son also does. For the Father loves the Son and shows him all he does."

John 5:19-20

God does not tolerate rivals—but he absolutely loves his Son. This was the key that the religious leaders failed to see. They saw in Jesus a direct competition to the unique glory of God and so they began to persecute him. They were deeply offended by the audacity of this humble carpenter from nowhere.

They almost had a point—there are countless times when mere human beings have tried to set themselves up as a rival to God. And God always brings them down. For example, the great king of Babylon, Nebuchadnezzar, had a go:

> *Is not this the great Babylon I have built as my royal residence, by my mighty power and for the glory of my majesty. (Daniel 4:30)*

Nebuchadnezzar spoke in god-talk. So, as a consequence, the one true God stripped him of his throne and sent him out to eat grass. No one in all of creation is worthy to stand alongside God and share his glory. But then comes Jesus, who clearly places himself as an equal to God. That seems outrageous but God did not stop him. Why?

The answer is simple and yet profound: Jesus is not a rival but a Son.

This language of Father and Son takes us deep into the mysteries of eternity. Before Jesus was born as a man, he was for ever existent as the Son. Before creation was spoken into being, there was an eternal Father and an eternal Son. This is why John is able to say that Jesus was with God (Son with the Father) and that Jesus was God (Son equal in glory with the Father). It doesn't solve all the problems or remove all our questions, but it does show us at least three beautiful things.

Firstly, God has always been the Father because he has always had the Son. God does not change. We change all the time—for 25 years of my life I was not a father, and then I had a son. But God is not like us, so there was no point in eternity when he became a father. This is called the eternal relations of the Father and Son. This relationship defines who God is now and who God has always been.

Secondly, it means that the Father is the source of the Son. The Father eternally generates the Son. There is an intimate and deep oneness between them. The Son is not a second being who exists independently from the Father. His being depends upon the Father.

Thirdly, it means that the Father has always loved the Son. God does not describe this relationship as a master and servant. Or a general and soldier. He reveals himself as Father and Son so that we catch something of the immense love between them.

Imagine a relationship so perfect that there is no suspicion, no competition, no misunderstanding, no disappointment, no division. A relationship so close that whatever the Father does, the Son also does. They are one and they work as one.

This is the God we adore. The God who is Father and Son (and also Holy Spirit, to paint the full picture!). It is a mystery beyond our comprehension, but it is not beyond our worship. When Jesus calls himself the Son, you can almost feel the Father's pleasure.

Jesus is wonderful because he has always existed in this stunning relationship of love. He needs nothing because he lacks nothing.

How does this idea of Jesus as the eternal Son lead you to worship today?

Radiance

The Son is the radiance of God's glory and the exact representation of his being, sustaining all things by his powerful word. After he had provided purification for sins, he sat down at the right hand of the Majesty in heaven.

Hebrews 1:3

Over the centuries, many writers have likened the Lord Jesus to the golden rays of sunshine. It is a beautiful image.

Sunshine is so powerful. It is able to pierce through the deepest darkness with a light that cannot be stopped. It drives away the lingering shadows of night. It floods the world with warmth, melting the icy chill of winter and bringing the sweet promise of summer. Sunshine is life-giving, joy-bringing, world-changing—it takes all the goodness of the sun and floods the earth with its smile.

A person who is trapped underground in a cave finds themselves in fearful darkness, untouched by light. The problem is not that the sun has stopped being glorious, but that in the cave there is no way to feel that goodness. The beauty of the sun is only experienced as rays of sunshine fall on our skin.

Just as the sun has the sunshine, so God has his Son.

God is infinitely more wonderful than the sun. His beauty is boundless and his majesty unparalleled. But God is in heaven and we are on earth—how could we ever bask in that glory?

The Son is the radiance of God's glory. (Hebrews 1:3)

The eternal Son of God is the means by which all the goodness of God is brought to every corner of this earth. The glory of God radiates out to us in the person of his Son. That is why we might rightly speak of Jesus as the sunshine of God. Jesus is the exact representation of God's glory; what we experience in him is truly the glory of God.

It is not like the bizarre human invention of sunbeds. We love the sun so much that we have tried to develop an artificial sunshine in order to top up the tan during the winter months. But lying in the harsh glare of a sunbed doesn't even compare to stretching out on the grass on a warm sunny day. It is a poor (and probably unhealthy) substitute.

Think what we have already seen: Jesus is the Word who is co-eternal with God. He is the Son who is in eternal relationship with his Father. He is of one essence and nature with God the Father and the Holy Spirit. Therefore, the glory with which he shines is the very glory of God himself.

It is ridiculous to try and somehow divide the sun from its rays. You cannot have one without the other. The sun in its very nature and being is continually generating the sunshine. The old Church Father Tertullian spoke of this idea when he wrote:

> *Even when the ray is shot from the sun, it is still part of the parent mass; the sun will still be in the ray, because it is a ray of the sun—there is no division of substance, but merely an extension.*

This means that we can bask in the true and essential glory of God as we come to Jesus the Son. All that is in God is carried to us in the person of Jesus. There is nothing more that God has for us—in fact, there is nothing more that God is, apart from what we find in Jesus.

Yet how quickly we turn to all sorts of other "sunbeds". We imagine that the glory we crave can be found elsewhere. We look for light and warmth and life outside of Christ but there is nothing there. Only a harsh and artificial glory that will never satisfy and will ultimately damage us.

Today, will you bask in the radiance of God's glory that we find in Jesus? All that God is, is yours in Christ. God holds nothing back but pours out himself in blessing upon you.

Jesus is the sunshine through whom we can experience and enjoy all the glory and goodness of God.

Are you seeking other sunshine to bring joy to your life? Are you settling for what is artificial and harmful? Make time to Son-bathe today.

I Am

Before Abraham was born, I am!

John 8:58

We all love heroes, and the Jewish nation were no different. They had some strong contenders, but it would be hard to imagine anyone greater than Abraham. He was the promise-receiving, nation-fathering, altar-building, son-not-withholding, astonishing man of faith. The whole nation traced its roots and history back to him.

Mentioning his name was a quick way to put people back in their place. *Are you greater than our father Abraham? No? Didn't think so. Now be quiet and go home.* In terms of human greatness, Abraham was as good as it would get.

So, when Jesus is rapidly growing in popularity, the religious leaders try to quieten things down. They decide to use the Abraham put-down on Jesus. "Are you greater than our father Abraham?" (John 8:53).

But instead of a sheepish silence, the carpenter from Nazareth gave the most scandalous reply. He took their Abraham question and raised it to a whole new level. Brace yourself:

Your father Abraham rejoiced at the thought of seeing my day; he saw it and was glad. (v 56)

Not just greater than Abraham, Jesus claims to be the object of Abraham's faith and the source of his deepest joy. When Abraham rejoiced in God's promises, he was rejoicing in Jesus. When Abraham pulled a ram out of a bush to sacrifice instead of his son, he was trusting in Jesus, the perfect Lamb of God. Abraham's hope was pinned on Jesus, even though he didn't know his name.

That is some answer. The religious leaders are having their world blown apart. They try a counteroffensive to gain back control and mockingly ask how Jesus could possibly have seen Abraham. But Jesus responds with an even greater bombshell:

Before Abraham was born, I am. (v 58)

This has dialled up to full volume—for the Jewish leaders, there is no missing what Jesus is saying. I AM is the very name of God. And Jesus applies it to himself: *I am the God that Abraham believed in.* You have to let that sink in and feel the majesty. The name of God is so infinitely precious. I AM is how God chose to introduce himself to Moses in Exodus 3 at the burning bush. And what a name it is—it magnifies God and humbles us.

It speaks of his *eternal existence.* To be human is to have a beginning—but not for God. He simply is. He always has been and always will be. He is pure existence. There was never a time when he was not.

It speaks of his *unchanging reality*. To be human is to become something that we currently are not (older, wiser, weaker, etc.). We are constantly changing. But God is not ageing. He is not growing. He is not learning. He does not change. God is solid ground in a world that shifts all around us.

It speaks of him as *the source of all that exists*. All existence flows from him and therefore is dependent on him. Nothing exists independently of God. We like to pretend in some way that our existence is what really matters—it isn't. God's existence is the heart of all things. That is what Abraham discovered: he was not interested in human greatness but in God's greatness.

Jesus takes this name as his own; he could not claim more for his identity. This is who we meet in the pages of the Gospels.

If you are thinking that Jesus did get older and did change and grow while on earth, you would be correct. We will get to that in section 3 when we explore him becoming human. But for now, we should stop on our journey to simply marvel at his eternal nature.

Before he ever became a man, Jesus was the I AM. Eternally existent, unchanging in nature, the source of all things. He silences all other claims to greatness.

Jesus is wonderful because he is the great I AM. We can stop with endless attempts to prove how great we are and instead rest in his greatness.

How does the greatness of Jesus make you feel small? How does he make you feel wonder?

First and Last

Do not be afraid. I am the First and the Last.

Revelation 1:17

When someone tells you, "Do not be afraid", it is because three things are true. Firstly, there is something lurking that has fear-inducing potential. Secondly, you share the natural human inclination towards fear. Thirdly, there is a state to live in that is better than living in fear.

But in the face of fear, you need more than just words. You need something solid that can actually remove the fear, and that is what Jesus is talking about in Revelation 1. He is not denying that there is real and present danger (unlike the dog owner who says, "Don't be afraid, he doesn't bite"). When we look at the reality of the world, fear is not a misplaced emotion. Jesus is not calling us to live in denial.

Neither does he mean, "Don't be afraid, you can do this" (as in, "Feel the fear and do it anyway"). When we look within ourselves and see our frailty and weakness, again, fear is not a misplaced emotion. Jesus is not calling us to a greater self-belief.

The antidote to fear is found in what Jesus says next. "I am the First and the Last." That is the fear-defeating reality that Jesus is inviting us to experience.

So how exactly does that help?

Fear is an obvious consequence of living lives that we cannot control. Time marches, disaster strikes, dreams fade, death stalks. Even when things are good, we fear what might be coming round the corner.

So, we grasp at anything that gives us a sense of control and order—anything that might provide stability and security. The problem is that, in the face of real danger and threat, these things are about as effective as a baby's comfort blanket. Our spreadsheets, insurance policies, pension pots, and job security are as fragile as a toddler's teddy. We need something more stable and solid. We need someone who sits outside of the chaos—out of the reach of death itself.

Now hear the words of Jesus thunder like a waterfall: "I am the First and the Last". The sheer majesty of those words is breathtaking. In one short sentence, Jesus effortlessly sweeps us from eternity to eternity. Stop and let it sink in. This is our God.

To be the First means nothing comes before you. Jesus never has to fight to prove his worth. He doesn't need the approval of the crowds. He is not challenged by rivals. He was there before it all. Whatever you might fear, whatever seems immovable and all-consuming, Jesus was there before it. The superpowers that arrogantly flex their muscles, the sicknesses that invade our bodies, the systems that perpetuate injustice, even the death that inevitably waits for us—none of these things are ultimate. Jesus was before them all. Do you feel the solid ground?

To be the Last means nothing will outlast you. Jesus will never be surpassed or replaced or upgraded. He will never be dethroned or defeated. He will never be a has-been or a quaint relic of history. He will never look back wistfully on the good old days. He will never sit in a rocking chair reminiscing about the past. When the boastful tongues of tyrants lie silenced in the grave, Jesus will still reign.

And in case we find ourselves doubting this reality, we have a tangible demonstration in history. The one who is the First and Last became like us. He took on our frail existence. Humanity tried to defeat him, Satan tried to dethrone him, death tried to finish him, but he rose in triumph. So he is rightly called by this name.

When we feel fear rising, rather than cling to temporary things that are uncertain and fickle, we need to hear the truth that Jesus is the First and the Last.

Jesus is wonderful because before anything else, he was there. And after everything else, he will still be there. Our lives shift and change, but Jesus doesn't.

What practically makes you feel safe in the world? How reliable is that thing you are trusting? How does the eternal reality of Jesus provide a firmer foundation?

Creator

For in him all things were created: things in heaven and on earth, visible and invisible, whether thrones or powers or rulers or authorities; all things have been created through him and for him.

Colossians 1:16

Truly great artists have two key attributes. Firstly, they have a creative genius that can imagine a reality which does not yet exist. And secondly, they have the creative power to bring into existence that which they imagined. This is what leads to the art, the music and the stories that move us and bring us joy. We celebrate this creativity.

But let me take you further back to an even greater genius. Imagine a creativity that could conceive of something when there was nothing at all. Human artists take the ideas, stories, patterns, and chords that have gone before and reimagine them in new and beautiful forms. But to start with nothing and conceive of something is a whole different level.

And then imagine the power to be able to bring that imagined world into existence out of nothing. A human painter might start with a blank canvas, but there is still a canvas. She has colours and textures. She has the world around her. She combines these things to create something new. But to create something out of nothing is impossible for even the most gifted of humans.

But all this is easy for God, the Creator—the creative genius and creative power that brought all other things into being. It is the most basic of all theological truths: God made you. God made everything. This reality has a double effect on us: it both humbles us (we are creatures) and honours us (we are created). Sometimes we act as if we are God. Sometimes we act as if we are worthless. We are neither.

But we are pursuing a deeper understanding of the Lord Jesus and so we must say more. The God who created us is not an impersonal force but the eternal Father. He brought all things into existence through his eternal Son. It was an overflow of the divine relationship.

You were created out of the joyful relationship of the Father and Son. The Son was not passively waiting for the moment when he would come as a baby. He is the means by which the Father executed his work of creation.

We find ourselves back at the fundamental reality of God as the Father, the Son and the Spirit. Not three gods with three wills who work in co-operation. But one God, with one nature, and one will who work inseparably. So, the Father creates, the Son creates, the Spirit creates—all in perfect unity and harmony. This has a number of important implications for us.

It means that creation does not flow from an aching pain in God that needed to be filled. Rather, God creates out of the pure joy of perfect love. God doesn't need us, but he does love us. Let that truth both humble you and honour you.

It also means that creation is not God's desperate attempt to prove his awesome power. It is not the terrifying insecurity of a tyrant. Rather creation is the controlled, gentle, awesome power flowing from the Father and the Son.

Perhaps we need to recapture the reality of Jesus as our Creator. That will surely mean humility. You are a creature that belongs to the one who made you. Will you acknowledge him today? It will also mean wide-eyed wonder that he chose to create us. When you see beauty, let that draw you back to worship the Creator. Walk through this world with your eyes open to all that the Lord Jesus has made. The one who died for you is the one who made all the good things you enjoy. Worship him for his creative genius and his power that brought the wonders of this world into existence.

Jesus is wonderful because the Father created all things through him. You are not a random accident, but you were created by the Lord Jesus.

Where do you find yourself becoming proud and boastful? Or where might you tend to feel worthless? How does the truth of Jesus as your Creator bring you joy today?

The Sustainer

He is before all things,
and in him all things hold together.

Colossians 1:17

When life is falling apart, our instinctive response is to try to hold things together. As the universe conspires against us, we desperately try to keep the show on the road—covering the cracks, putting on a brave face, keeping the plates spinning. We walk into church whispering to ourselves, "I just need to hold it together".

How many tears have been shed? How much sleep has been lost? How many people have been crushed by the unimaginable burden of "holding things together"?

Here is the liberating truth you need today: that is not your job. From all eternity past, Jesus is the one who has been holding it all together. Actively, deliberately, powerfully and constantly. He is sustaining all things.

Feel the burden on your shoulders start to lift. Breathe in this wonderful truth.

We cannot settle for a passive view of God; that would be a worldview called deism. It goes something like this: God created all things, wound his creation up like a children's toy, and then stepped back to watch it all unfold. In this view, the natural laws of science mean that God is not needed on a day-to-day basis. He might need to step in from time to time if there is a problem that needs fixing, but otherwise it carries on under its own steam.

The Bible portrays things so very differently. Here are some of the active ways that the Bible says that God is sustaining all things right now:

- All creatures are looking to him for their daily food (Psalm 104:27).
- Every single moment of life and breath comes from him (Acts 17:25).
- The stars only appear in the night sky because he calls them by name (Isaiah 40:26).

I could go on and on. The stars come out. The baby cries. The blackbird eats the worm. It isn't just the way things are—it is the active work of God in our everyday world. Open your eyes and see God's hand in every moment of every day.

This is what God has been doing from the beginning. That means this is what the eternal Son of God has been doing ever since creation burst forth. He has been constantly watching, holding, caring, providing, protecting and preserving this world. He does that for the whole cosmos. And he does it for you.

When things are going our way, this is easier to see. But it takes the eyes of faith to see it is still true on the darkest days. He is still sustaining you. He is still for you. He has not abandoned you.

If we simply think of Jesus as a figure from history, we will miss the eternal comfort that we can find in him. He really was a baby born in a manger, but at the very same time he was also holding the planets in their orbits and feeding the great creatures of the deep. As he gently touched the eyes of the blind man and showed such love and compassion, it was still through him that the billions of galaxies took their place.

As his enemies shouted "Crucify" and hurled their insults at him, he was the one who enabled each breath they took and each beat of their hearts. Can you imagine the sheer grace and power it would take to sustain those who would cause you such pain? The creatures murder the very one upon whom their lives depend, and they didn't even realise. Their work was done, they went home that night, and they ate the food that he had provided.

From all eternity, the Lord Jesus has been the one in whom all things hold together. Remove him and it all unravels and falls apart. This is true for the universe and it is true of our individual lives too.

Jesus is wonderful because he is sustaining you right now. Whether you are worshipping or sinning, he is sustaining you. You don't have to hold it all together. He is doing that.

In what ways do you feel like things are falling apart? Perhaps personally or on a world stage? How does it help you today to know that Jesus is the Sustainer? Chew on that and enjoy this truth for a few moments today.

Chosen

He was chosen before the creation of the world, but was revealed in these last times for your sake.

1 Peter 1:20

I am not much of a chess player, but I can appreciate the beauty of the game. You need great skill and strategic planning. But you also need the ability to react to the moves your opponent makes. It's a slow-motion dance that is full of suspense. The story plays out and you don't know who will win.

Chess is like a mini version of our human story. Our existence is a constant dance of making plans and then reacting to the ever-changing set of circumstances that is placed in our path. Things take us by surprise, things frustrate us; we have hopes and dreams but we are constantly having to react and change. We don't know what is coming round the corner.

It is easy to assume that God operates the same way. Although he has his plans for the world and although he is very powerful, we imagine that he doesn't know what humanity might do next. So, he waits and reacts to what is thrown at him. He is part of this same dance—hoping, planning, reacting. Even if we are pretty confident that he will ultimately win, the route to be taken into the future is still unknown.

The reality we find in the Bible is very different. The apostle Peter wrote that Jesus Christ was chosen before the creation of the world. Before there were planets and trees, people and kings. Before there was sin and injustice, death and fear. Before the world was in a desperate mess in need of a Redeemer. Before all of that, Peter says that Christ was already chosen by God to put everything right.

This is significant because it means that God's actions in this world are not reactive but proactive. We are not part of a cosmic game of chess where each player waits for the other to make a move. God has always had a plan, and it always revolved around Jesus.

The word "chosen" involves the idea of being foreknown. It was already known that Christ would be the one who would redeem the world by his blood. That means it was already known that the world would need redeeming. Christ was already the designated Redeemer. This is highly significant to our understanding of the person of Jesus.

When human beings rebelled against God, it did not take him by surprise. He did not have to alter anything in his plan. When sin and death devastated God's beautiful creation, it was a tragedy but it was not a disaster. God is grieved by human sin but also fully knows its consequences.

What was Jesus chosen for? He was chosen to be the Redeemer. It was already known that his blood would be poured out. It was already known that God would sacrifice the most costly thing.

Theologians talk about the covenant of redemption: the Father, Son and Holy Spirit, eternally covenanted with one another to create and then redeem the world. It was always the Son who was going to be the Redeemer. Before the creation of the world, it was already fixed and decided in the eternal counsel of God.

This is majestic and extraordinary love; this is glory beyond imagination. God created the world knowing that it would cost the death of his Son to redeem and restore.

God is not waiting to see what we do and then reacting accordingly. He is far above all things. He already foreknew. He already chose Christ. He already had his plan.

We may have all sorts of questions about why God does things the way he does them. From our earthly perspective, we might even find ourselves questioning what he is doing. But if the Lord Jesus was chosen before the creation of the world to redeem us by his precious blood, then we can find a resting place. God is not just trying his best—he is not making things up as he goes along. He is working out his eternal purpose through Jesus.

Jesus is wonderful because, before the world was created, he was already chosen to be the Redeemer. God is not surprised by all that has happened. He is working out his plan that from all eternity has been agreed with his Son.

When do you feel like God has lost control or is fighting a losing battle? How does the eternal plan of God to redeem the world bring you hope?

9

The Lamb

The Lamb who was slain from the creation of the world.

Revelation 13:8

The early church was caught up in a terrifying and chaotic time. There was persecution and suffering. There was danger and threat. The church looked weak and fragile but there was something bigger going on: the book of Revelation pulls back the curtain to give us a glimpse of eternal truths.

In chapter 13, we see a beast that is a hideous combination of dangerous animals that hunt and destroy their prey without mercy. This represents human leaders abusing authority to gain status and power. If that isn't bad enough, behind this ruthless political power stands the even more sinister figure of the dragon, who is the devil—the great enemy of God and his people. And the greatest tragedy of all is that the world is completely captivated by it. People worship at the altar of power and scramble for a piece of it.

No wonder the church is so battered and trampled in this great stampede. But our eternal comfort and divine hope are found in the eternal purposes and plans of God. As the whole world worships the beast, the church is described as those whose names have been written in the Lamb's book of life—"the Lamb who was slain from the creation of the world" (v 8, ESV).

We find ourselves once again transported from the turbulent battles of history and lifted into the divine counsel of eternity to see the covenant of redemption that God has put in place. Not only was Christ chosen before the creation of the world, but he was also already appointed as the slain Lamb.

It is surely significant that the eternal hope in the face of a vicious beast is a slain Lamb. Here is the kingdom of God in all its beautiful contrast to the kingdoms of this world. This is a theme we will keep returning to. Crushing enemies are not defeated by a hero who can out-crush them—the vicious beasts of this world will be brought down by the slain Lamb.

It would be hard to think of a weaker, more helpless creature than a lamb. It has no power or strength. It has no shrewdness or speed. Yet, it is the Lamb that confounds the cunning of the serpent and undermines the power of the dragon.

Jesus is that Lamb, but what does it mean that he was slain before the creation of the world?

It means that Jesus coming as the Lamb of God was not a desperate response to human sin but an eternal decision in the will of God. It means that the very heart of God has always been a heart of humble sacrifice rather than a heart of crushing power.

When you meet a lamb in the Bible, it normally has only one purpose: it will be slain. The life of the lamb will be poured out in order that someone else will live. This is sacrifice—the most powerful dynamic in the universe. God repeatedly taught this principle to his people through the sacrificial system in the temple. Thousands of lambs were slain, each one teaching the same thing. This is not a picture of barbaric violence, rather, we are being shown that sacrificial love lies at the very heart of God's purpose for his world.

Before lambs had ever been created, Jesus was already the Lamb. Before the first lamb was ever sacrificed, the death of the true Lamb was already sealed.

Human history is a story of violence and chaos. Beast-like powers have battled it out for supremacy. Many people have been caught up in the crossfire and crushed along the way. But the beasts will never win; proud, rebellious dictators will be brought down.

And the reason why? The Lamb was slain before the creation of the world and his humble sacrificial love is the ultimate power that will bring all other powers to an end.

The song that will be sung for all eternity is simple: *worthy is the Lamb who was slain.*

Jesus is wonderful because he is the Lamb who was slain before the creation of the world. All God's grace to this world is because of his sacrifice.

How does this eternal truth bring peace to your heart today?

Firstborn

The firstborn over all creation.

Colossians 1:15

There are basically two ways to gain status in this world—either it is bestowed on you as an inheritance (think of the royal family) or you earn it through your own hard work (think of the self-made billionaire).

Which system do you instinctively prefer?

The fact that some are born into privilege feels unfair and arbitrary. It often means that people end up with a status that they do not deserve. Power is highly controlled by the elite and protected at all costs. It feels old-fashioned, outdated and wrong.

The idea of a meritocracy might feel instinctively better but when you think about it, this method also carries huge dangers. It can create a harsh culture where the weakest are crushed in the great scramble for the top. It is a dog-eat-dog world where power ends up in the hands of the strongest and most ruthless. We can find ourselves living with the constant pressure to prove our worth. It increases the likelihood of insecurity and anxiety and it can lead to arrogance and pride.

So, which is truly better: status that is inherited or status that is earned?

Perhaps the problem lies deeper. Whichever way you slice the pie, human beings have a terrible track record when it comes to positions of power. High status is an intoxicating drug for the human heart. Whether we inherited it or earned it, we all have a habit of misusing it.

God's wisdom subverts both of these ways of thinking; he continually acts to defy all human wisdom and systems.

The firstborn son historically had a significant difference in status and honour to subsequent children in a family. But the Old Testament shows a backstory that undermines the human order and way of thinking. Firstly, we should notice that the "natural" rights of the firstborn son are often overturned in the Bible. Time and again it is not the firstborn in the family that receives God's blessing—the order is reversed. There is a long line of firstborns who were rejected in favour of the younger: Cain, Ishmael, Esau, Reuben, and so the list goes on.

God is teaching us that his view of the firstborn is not what we might naturally expect. He does not follow human ideas of power. He chooses the younger and weaker and elevates them to the higher place. You can sense the human categories shifting out of joint and toes being stepped on.

Secondly, the title of firstborn is given to the nation of Israel: "This is what the Lord says: Israel is my *firstborn* son" (Exodus 4:22). God bestowed this special status on his people as his gift to them. It gave them a great privilege in the world; they belonged to God. But the problem was that this privilege caused them to become proud. They abused their position and thought of themselves as superior to the nations around them. That was never the point, but privilege so often leads to pride.

So, who could ever be trusted with the title of "firstborn over all creation"? Who could ever be entrusted with such honour and status? Who could ever occupy this highest of all positions?

Look at the figure hanging dead on a cross and you will find your answer. It is not the one who grasps for power but the one who gives it all away; not the one the world applauds but the one who embraces weakness; not the one who demands his rights but the one who gives them up. Jesus is the one who has eternally been the firstborn over all creation—not meaning that he was the first to be created but that he is the one who is worthy of the highest status.

The Father has bestowed on Jesus this greatest of all honours. The Father has subverted all our categories of status and power. Come and behold the beauty of the firstborn over all creation.

Jesus is wonderful because he alone can be trusted with the position of highest honour.

Where do you see an unhealthy attitude towards status taking root in your heart? How can you confess this and address it in the light of Jesus' humility and his honour?

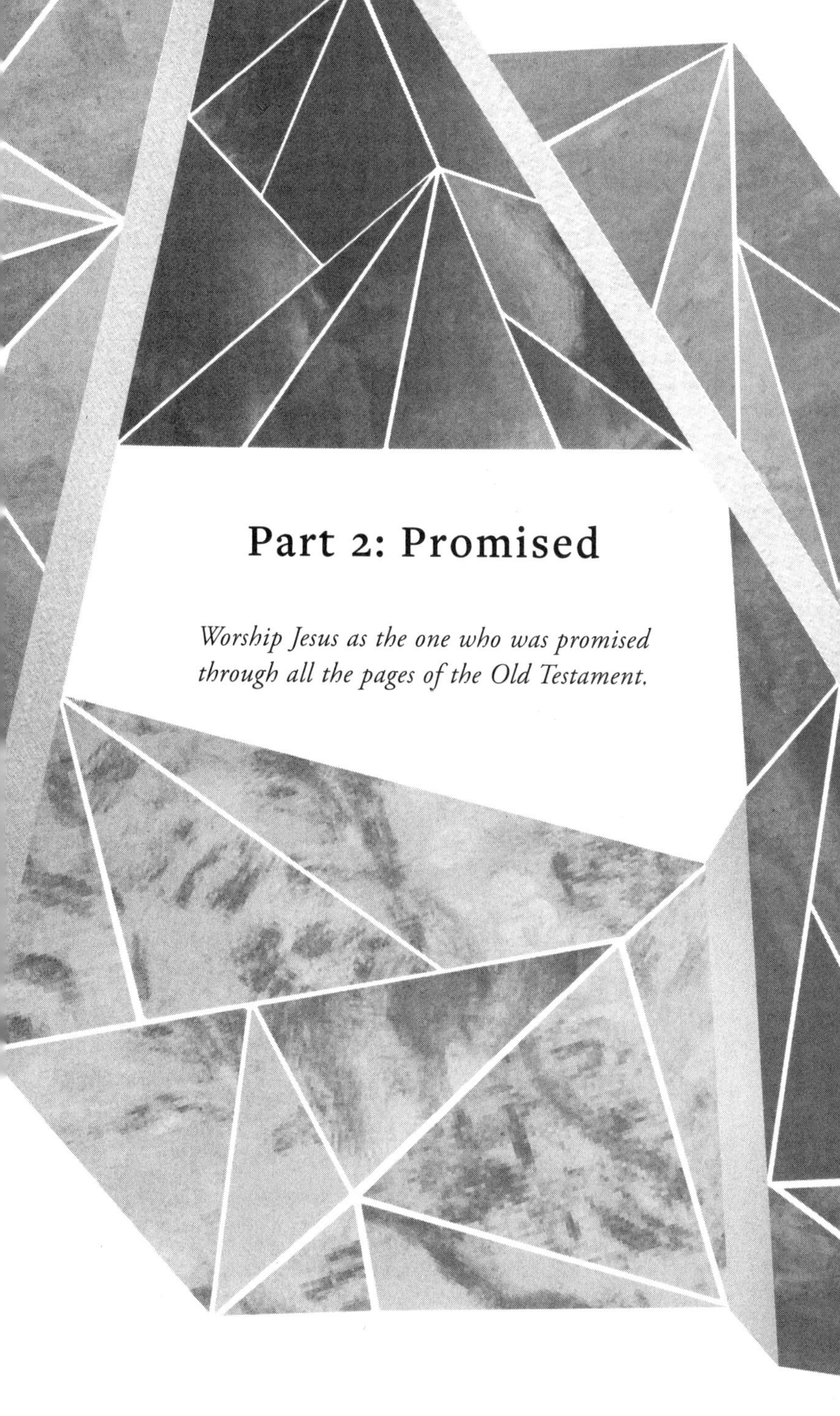

Part 2: Promised

Worship Jesus as the one who was promised through all the pages of the Old Testament.

The Seed

The promises were spoken to Abraham and to his seed.

Galatians 3:16

The whole Bible story rests on the promise that God made to Abraham. It is breathtaking in its simplicity: God appeared to him in Genesis 12 and said, "I will…"

When someone says, "I will" it brings into existence something brand new. Think of a bride and groom on their wedding day—they say these two words and create a new reality. Two little words produce a binding, legal, covenant relationship. They are not words we should utter carelessly or lightly.

So it is with the great and precious promises of God. He owes us nothing. He is under no obligation to us. He is the Creator, and as such it is we who owe him worship and thanks. And yet, God freely chose to make the first move. When he said, "I will bless you", the world changed.

This is why the relationship between God and his people can so often be described in terms of a marriage. He binds himself to Abraham under the obligation of a promise. Notice this carefully: before God makes any demands on his people, before there are any laws and commands, and without any conditions or clauses, God says to Abraham, "I will". He takes all the responsibility onto himself. This is magnificent kindness. This is the covenant of grace.

Let's be clear—there was nothing special about Abraham. At the time of the promise, he was worshipping idols in a far-off land. He did not know the Creator, yet God chose him. In fact, it is the ordinariness of the choice that makes it so stunning. He was not a brave knight or a wise teacher or a wealthy ruler or a mighty king. He was not the best that humanity had to offer. He was a nobody, and that is the point of God's choice.

A relationship with God does not start when we have done enough to gain his attention. No, it all goes back to this one moment when God stooped down to speak to Abraham and made this world-changing promise. It is God who takes all of the initiative and all of the obligation. The rest of the Bible is the story of God keeping this covenant promise.

All of this is very good but there's more that we need to see here. This is not simply a promise to Abraham. The apostle Paul reflects back on this moment and says that "the promises were spoken to Abraham and to his seed" (Galatians 3:16). This is not an unusual thought; all of Abraham's offspring (seed) have a claim on the promise. But then comes the twist...

Paul explicitly clarifies that by "seed" he is talking about *one* person—not all of Abraham's offspring. The promises were spoken to two individuals: Abraham and Christ.

This is monumental. When you put this together with all that we have seen about the eternal nature of the Son of God, it opens up a whole new understanding of God's covenant. As God spoke to Abraham, we should hear God the Father making a covenant promise to his Son.

Listen to the promises of Genesis 12 as God the Father speaking directly to his beloved eternal Son:

I will make you into a great nation,
and I will bless you;
I will make your name great,
and you will be a blessing;
... all peoples on earth
will be blessed through you. (v 2-3)

Do you hear it? In that moment Abraham is caught up in the eternal covenant of the Father and the Son. It was always about Jesus. It was always about his name and his blessing. It was always through him that blessing would come to the world.

The human story of Abraham's family is one of unfaithfulness and failure. They trash the great covenant promises of God; they are unfaithful. But it was never ultimately about them—it was always about Christ. Why did God not give up on his unfaithful people? Why did he not abandon the promise? Why did he not scrap it all and start again?

It is all because the unbreakable promise that God made to Abraham was actually an unbreakable promise to his Son. Look at the eternal security that gives us. Our relationship with God, the blessing of all the nations, our purpose in the world, and the great plan of God to put things right does not depend on our performance and merit but on the extraordinary promise that the Father has made to his Son. We are caught up in that promise. That is our privilege—it is ours by grace.

Jesus is wonderful because the Father has made unbreakable promises to him that will result in blessing for all the nations of the world.

How does it change your perspective to know that God places demands on himself before he places demands on us? How does it help you to feel secure, knowing that all God's blessing rests on the promise he has made to his Son (the seed of Abraham)?

12

The Prophet

I will raise up for them a prophet like you
from among their fellow Israelites.

Deuteronomy 18:18

Words are incredibly precious. They enable us to take what is hidden within us and let others into that reality. Every time you speak to someone it creates the possibility of relationship. It may just be a fleeting moment as you apologise to a stranger for bumping into them on the street. Or it may be an occasion of profound depth as you open your heart to a dear friend.

But what about God? Does God speak? We might instinctively say yes, of course. But perhaps it isn't so obvious. It depends on how we view God. If we mean a god who is just a spiritual force directing the universe, then there would be no expectation that he or it would speak. Or if we imagine a god who is distant and disinterested, once again, we'd be left without a word. That would be a devastating existence. No way to know God. No relationship.

Take a moment to consider the darkness of a world where there is no word from God. We could guess, we could reason, we could argue, we could observe, but we could never fully *know*. Now, open your heart in worship and delight as you encounter the God who speaks. He speaks and creates the world. He speaks and blesses his creation. He speaks to commission his creatures and to rule and to reveal. It is relentless on page after page of the Bible—God speaks.

Speaking creates relationship. Speaking establishes relationship. Speaking maintains relationship.

This is why the role of prophet was so central and precious for the people of God. It was through the prophets that God chose to speak his word to his world. Although God spoke in all sorts of ways, the voice of the prophet emerges as the primary way that God communicates to the people. This is significant because it means that God's word is not a distant, disembodied voice from the sky but an embodied word that comes near to us in the person of the prophet.

Moses is the first of the prophets and the pattern is set for all who will follow. From Moses to Jeremiah, from Micah to Obadiah, God appoints prophets to be his mouthpiece. The prophetic dynamic is spelled out plainly when God says to Jeremiah, "I have put my words in your mouth" (Jeremiah 1:9). It is the divine word in a human mouth; the living, close, precious word of God.

It is the word of the prophet that sets slaves free, expresses glorious love, warns the rebellious, reveals glory, establishes a covenant and gives beautiful laws. What was hidden deep in the heart of God is poured out so that we could understand the truth. We don't have to guess what God is like—he has spoken through his prophets. They wrote down what was revealed to them in order that the prophetic word might continue to feed and instruct God's people.

But right from the start, Moses knew that a greater Prophet would one day come. He spells it out in Deuteronomy 18—God will raise up another Prophet like Moses. And so the people watch and wait. Many prophets come and go. They speak the word of God, but none of them could be considered as the greater Moses.

Until… a murmuring crowd who had been captivated by the words and deeds of Jesus began to whisper the ancient promise:

> *Surely this is the Prophet who is to come into the world.*
> *(John 6:14)*

The great prophetic hope finds the fulfilment it was crying out for. Now the word of God is heard perfectly from the mouth of the perfect human being. The word of God is embodied in flesh. The heart of God is now perfectly revealed in the greatest Prophet. God has spoken, and that means relationship is possible, God is knowable, and we can be sure about what is true.

Jesus is the one who speaks the words of life. Jesus is the one whose words are slavery-smashing, joy-bringing, rebel-warning, covenant-establishing, God-revealing. Those words have been perfectly recorded for us in the Bible so that we might hear the voice of God and live.

You don't have to guess anymore. Come to Jesus and you can know.

Jesus is wonderful because he is the last and greatest Prophet—the embodied Word of God. He speaks so that we can know God. He doesn't come to confuse or obscure truth but to make God plain to us so that we might know and worship him.

In what way do you take for granted that God speaks? When do you find yourself not listening?

The King

The Lord God will give him
the throne of his father David.

Luke 1:32

There is an important distinction between what we want and what we need. We all know this. It is why we feed children broccoli when they are asking for chocolate. But even if we know it, we can still be painfully slow to learn.

By the end of the book of Judges, it is very clear that the people of Israel desperately need a king. Just look at the mess they are in:

> *In those days Israel had no king; everyone did as they saw fit. (Judges 21:25)*

This is why the book of Ruth follows Judges in the Bible. It is not a random love story floating in space. It is the story of how God will give Israel the king they need. It is the family history of King David.

But the people are not yet ready for the king they *need.* They have a better plan. They are busy pursuing the king they *want.* Like children in a playground, they were looking at all the cool nations and wanted to be just like them. *We want a king like they have got.* They are thinking of someone impressive, strong and intimidating—someone who will make the other nations sit up and notice them.

The prophet Samuel warns them of what a "king like the nations" will do. He will take from them. He will burden them. He will be a disaster. But, like a child who refuses to believe that a chocolate-only diet is bad news, they still demand to have a king.

It is heartbreaking. The very identity of Israel was precisely that they were *not* like the nations around them. No one else had the Lord as their God. He went before them; he fought their battles; he protected and provided for them. But they just wanted to be like the other kids in the playground.

So God gives them King Saul. Here is the king they want: he is a head taller than anyone else, he is easily the best-looking man in Israel. He is impressive and will be a match for any of the kings around them. But despite all the hope and the hype, it is a disaster. Saul doesn't fear God. He does what seems right to himself. He becomes increasingly power-hungry and desperate. He just does not deliver. And it all ends in a shameful death in battle. A king like the nations was never what they needed.

So now the ground is prepared and the stage is set for God to teach his people what a true king looks like. When

God chose Saul, he gave the people what they wanted. When God chose David, he gave the people what they needed. He had already laid this out many centuries earlier in Deuteronomy 17. The king is not to build a massive army (v 16), accumulate treasure or wives (v 17) or set himself above the people (v 20). He is to fear God and lead the people in joyfully following God's law (v 18-19) rather than giving in to their idol-loving hearts. After the disaster of Saul, God now sets his heart upon David.

He is the youngest of eight brothers—remember the pattern we saw with the firstborn. He is a shepherd boy. He is a man who fears and trusts God. When he goes out to fight Goliath, everyone laughs at him. But he shows the people what it looks like to stand by faith in God's strength not human power. The king wins the victory, and all the people rejoice.

David is the first true king but he is not the final one. God promised David that through his family there would be a King who would come and rule in perfect righteousness for ever. The kings that followed David were disappointing. In fact, it got so bad that it looked like it was all over—but still the fragile line of David continued. The promise of God stood firm. The psalmists sang about this hope. The prophets pointed to this hope. The people waited for this hope. Where was the King, the Christ, the Messiah?

Then in the tiny town of Nazareth, an angel appeared to a young girl called Mary. He told her that she would give birth to a baby who would be given the throne of David for ever.

The King had finally arrived.

Jesus is not the King we might naturally want, but he is the King we desperately need. The people of his day rejected him. He had no army; he had no wealth; he looked so weak. At the cross, they nailed a sign that said, "The King of the Jews". He didn't look like any human king, but he came to be the King we need. What appeared to be weakness was the great moment of triumph. Our King defeated the enemies of sin and death and then rose again to reign for ever.

The world will still laugh at him. The world will still seek something more impressive. But if your heart aches for a king who will fight for you, serve you, give his life for you and then rise to lead you into true worship, then Jesus is precisely the King you're looking for.

Jesus is wonderful because he is the King we need, fulfilling all of the promises and hopes of the Old Testament prophets.

Where do you feel your desperate need of Jesus as your King today? Take some time to worship him and put your hope in him alone.

14

The Priest

... because Jesus lives forever
he has a permanent priesthood.

Hebrews 7:24

Fire presents us with a strange paradox. It both captivates us and terrifies us; it is beautiful and yet devastating. We find ourselves driven back and at the same time drawn closer.

In the Bible, the presence of God is often associated with a burning purity. This obviously presents a pretty serious threat to sinful humanity. You see it clearly in Exodus 24: the people come to Mount Sinai to meet with God—which sounds wonderful. But it isn't quite that straightforward. When God appears, we are told that "to the Israelites the glory of the LORD looked like a consuming fire on top of the mountain" (v 17).

You don't mess around with that sort of thing. You certainly wouldn't be running up the mountain to get closer, but you also wouldn't be able to pull your eyes away. Can you imagine that experience? Here is the key question we are left asking: How can the God of consuming fire also be the one who dwells with his people? How can we draw close to the very God whose purity drives us back?

The partial answer is found in the person of the priest. In Exodus 24, there is one person who is called to go up the mountain and enter the cloud of burning fire. How is it possible for a human being to enter the burning presence of God and not be consumed?

It is because Moses is chosen by God for this (highly dangerous) task of being a priest. The priest goes where no one else can go. The priest goes on behalf of all the people. This is the only way that God and humanity can ever come into contact. So Moses goes up the mountain and the consuming glory of God covers him.

The stakes could hardly be any higher—the destiny of a nation rests on his shoulders. If Moses is consumed by the burning fire of God, then there is no hope for the people at the bottom of the mountain. But Moses is not consumed; he is welcomed by God. The fact that there is a man in the presence of God gives hope for everyone.

God does not withdraw from sinful people and keep his distance. He provides the priest to be the bridge.

What happened on the mountain was only the start; it set the pattern for all the priests who would follow Moses. Year after year, a high priest was chosen from among the people. He was to be anointed with special oil and wear specific clothes. He was to offer sacrifices. And once a year he was to enter the Most Holy Place to make atonement for sin. The astonishing hope for the people is that yearly a human being entered the presence of God and was not consumed—the priest stood on their behalf.

The priest was a great comfort, but to enjoy true closeness with God it was always going to need more. The people were still left at the bottom of the mountain. The presence of God was still out of reach for the average person. But imagine a priest who could lead all of us into the holy presence of God—Jesus is that Priest and he is spectacular.

The Bible book of Hebrews contains an extended meditation on the work of Jesus as the great High Priest. Here are some of the things it says:

- He was without sin—unlike all the others who were part of the problem (4:15).
- He is the Priest for ever—unlike all the others who died (7:17, 21).
- He has entered the Most Holy Place of heaven itself—unlike the earthly sanctuary of the earthly priests (9:24).
- He offered his own blood to make atonement—unlike the blood of bulls and goats that cannot take away sin (9:12).
- He has made a once-for-all sacrifice—unlike the endless repeating rituals of the priests (7:27).
- He has cleansed us inwardly—unlike the priests who could only make people outwardly clean (9:14).
- He has made us holy so that we too may enter the Most Holy Place of God. We no longer stay at the bottom of the mountain but now with boldness can enter into the very presence of God (10:19; 4:16).

We may feel unworthy and unclean. We may feel excluded and distant. But Jesus our Priest has opened the way into God's presence. He has offered the sacrifice that makes you clean. He welcomes you to come near.

Jesus is wonderful because he stands in the presence of God on our behalf. We will not be consumed because Jesus is our perfect Priest. He has made atonement and opened the way.

Where do you feel unworthy to enter God's presence? How does Jesus our Priest give you hope today?

The Gate

I am the gate;
whoever enters through me will be saved.

John 10:9

A gate is a powerful thing. Some are small and wooden, others are grand and imposing, but every gate performs a mighty function. It stands as the connection point between two worlds. That might sound a little over dramatic but go with it for a moment. Think of the difference between a gate and a fence.

We put up fences to create boundaries and to separate different realms. Fences are designed to keep things apart and to keep people out. We put fences around our gardens because we do not want anyone and everyone trampling through our roses. But we don't want to keep *everybody* out, so at one point in the fence there is a gate. The fence separates; the gate connects.

An open gate is an invitation to enter. It is an offer to leave one world and enter a new one.

This is why gates have the power to create such strong emotions in us. I still remember the deep joy that flooded my heart as I approached the small wooden gate that stood at the top of the steps leading down into my granny's garden. The gate was the connection between the world without granny and the world with her. All of us will have gates we can think of that create a whole range of emotions in us (and not always positive!).

In the Old Testament, there is a fascinating account where a man called Jacob has an experience of God that ends with him saying, "This is the gate of heaven" (Genesis 28:17).

What does that mean?

Heaven and earth were originally created with a great deal of overlap. In Eden, God would come and walk in the garden in the cool of the day. No boundary, no fence, just open access. But when sin entered the world, a great separation opened up between heaven and earth. A fence was put in place that could not be crossed. It looked like the relationship was all over.

Yet there were moments in the Old Testament when there still appeared to be a connection point between heaven and earth. There were brief (and often strange) experiences when a connection was glimpsed. That is what happened to Jacob during a very strange night in a little place called Bethel.

He had a dream where he saw a "stairway resting on the earth, with its top reaching to heaven" (Genesis 28:12). Jacob is on the run from his brother and feels abandoned and alone, but in this dream God was showing Jacob the nearness of heaven to earth. The closeness that sin destroyed is somehow being re-established. It is an exceptional moment.

Jacob wakes up from his dream and says that he has glimpsed the gate of heaven. It is tantalising in its closeness and yet distant in its dreaminess. Is it real? Is it possible that there could be a gate between heaven and earth?

It is a puzzling story that hangs in the air and cries out for someone to come and make sense of it. As the years go by it becomes a distant memory. Until, hundreds of years later, Jesus utters these words:

> *I am the gate; whoever enters through me will be saved.*
> *(John 10:9)*

The late-night experience of Jacob suddenly comes crashing into very sharp focus. There is a connection point between the things above and the world below. What was dreamy and ethereal has become real and solid. It is not a place or a building or a magic portal—it is a person. Jesus is the Gate who connects heaven and earth. You come through him, and you enter heaven itself.

This is remarkably good news. Heaven is not a faraway place in a faraway land; it has come so near. Heaven is not just a future place that we go to when we die. It is God's dwelling place now and the gateway to enter is through Jesus. We are not abandoned and alone. We can know God today as we come to Jesus. We can experience God today as we come to Jesus. We can taste heaven today as we come to Jesus.

One day the great reunion of heaven and earth will be completed. Heaven will come down and we will live with

God in a new heaven and a new earth. But for now, praise God, there is a Gate.

Jesus is wonderful because he is the Gate who connects heaven and earth. We can know the nearness of God today as we come through Jesus.

How does this connection between heaven and earth create a deeper longing for you to know more of that closeness today?

16

The Rock

They drank from the spiritual rock that accompanied them, and that rock was Christ.

1 Corinthians 10:4

The sun above blazed down on them. The ground under their feet was hard and dry. They were desperately thirsty and there was no water—anywhere. The people became anxious and restless as imminent death filled their horizon. So they turned on Moses, their leader, and demanded:

"Give us water to drink."

Moses replied, "Why do you quarrel with me? Why do you put the Lord to the test?" (Exodus 17:2)

It is an absurd demand. How could Moses possibly do that? It is also an arrogant demand. Who do they think they are to be barking out commands? Plus, it is an outrageous demand. Have they forgotten God's amazing power and kindness when he led them out of slavery? Rather than turn to God in humble dependence, instead they stamp their feet and issue their orders to Moses.

It has only been a few months since they walked through the Red Sea and already they are in deep rebellion against the God who rescued them. They reject God and his kindness. They deserve nothing less than to be struck down by the mighty hand of God.

But God doesn't strike them down; he doesn't destroy them. Instead, he provides water for an absurd, arrogant and outrageous people. Right there, in the desert of death, life pours forth. And to make it even more wonderful, the source of this water is a rock. Not an underground spring or a plump cactus or a refreshing downpour of rain. Water gushes out of solid stone. It would be hard to think of a more unlikely and unpromising source, yet from the rock God brings life.

The choice of a rock is not without meaning—it is key to understanding this story. Look carefully at what God says to Moses:

> *I will stand there before you by the rock at Horeb. Strike the rock, and water will come out of it for the people to drink. (v 6)*

There are two key things to notice about this rock. Firstly, God comes and stands right alongside it. He is in front of the people on the rock. We are supposed to understand that the rock is becoming a visible representation of the presence of God. He identifies himself with it.

Secondly, Moses is told to strike the rock. If we have understood where God is standing, this becomes a shocking reality. As Moses lifts up his staff of judgment it is very clear who deserves to be struck down. The miserable and grumbling people of God deserve to fall in the desert for their rebellion. But instead, the staff strikes the rock of God's presence. As God is struck, life flows out from the rock to the rebellious and undeserving people.

As they gulped down the refreshing water that satisfied their aching thirst, little did they realise the true significance of what was happening. They were being refreshed and sustained by Christ himself. Many years before he would walk the earth, he was already the source of spiritual nourishment for his thirsty people. That is what Paul is telling us when he writes:

> *They drank from the spiritual rock that accompanied them, and that rock was Christ. (1 Corinthians 10:4)*

The presence of God in the rock was nothing less than the presence of Christ. As the rod of divine judgment struck the rock, it was striking Christ. It anticipated, with glorious hope, that one day this Rock would come in person. He would be struck at the cross, his side would be torn open and water would flow out to offer life to anyone who is thirsty.

When we read of the grumbling Israelites, we should surely see ourselves. We can be just as absurd in the demands that we make. We can be just as arrogant. We can be outrageous in how quickly we forget all that God has done for us. We can turn to all sorts of things that we think will satisfy our thirst and give us life. Can you see how deeply rebellion lurks in our hearts?

But there is glorious good news. Although we deserve to be struck, Jesus is the Rock who was struck for us so that streams of living water might flow from him and turn us from death to life. Come and drink deeply and find life that will satisfy.

Jesus is wonderful because he is the Rock who was struck to give life to our thirsty souls. As we drink from him, we are simply following in the footsteps of our forefathers who drank from the rock.

How do you feel thirsty and dissatisfied today? Will you bring that to Jesus and ask that he would be your all-satisfying living water?

The Shepherd

I am the good shepherd.

John 10:11

The job description of a shepherd is pretty simple. There are basically three responsibilities: lead the sheep, feed the sheep and protect the sheep. These tasks correspond precisely to the three fundamental shortcomings that sheep experience: they get lost, they get hungry and they get attacked. Sheep might be cute, but they are not well designed for a life of rugged independence in the big wide world. It's pretty clear that to be a sheep without a shepherd is not a life of joyful freedom but a life of terrible danger.

God knows that his people share a lot in common with sheep. They too face the triple threat of becoming lost, growing hungry and facing attack. So, because God loves his people very deeply, he provides them with leaders who are to be shepherds to the flock. Good leaders will mean safe sheep. Bad leaders will spell disaster.

God takes this whole thing very seriously. He really loves his sheep and so this really matters. Listen to the force of his accusation against the bad leaders of Israel:

> *Woe to you shepherds of Israel who only take care of yourselves! Should not shepherds take care of the flock? You eat the curds, clothe yourselves with the wool and slaughter the choice animals, but you do not take care of the flock. You have not strengthened the weak or healed those who are ill or bound up the injured. You have not brought back the strays or searched for the lost. You have ruled them harshly and brutally. So they were scattered because there was no shepherd, and when they were scattered they became food for all the wild animals.*
>
> *(Ezekiel 34:2-5)*

On every single front the shepherds have failed. They have not fed, led or protected the flock. God is angry with these useless shepherds. It is a tragic reality that there have been many since who have been entrusted with positions of leadership in the church and have harmed the sheep in their care. God reserves his strongest warnings for bad shepherds. He will remove them from his flock.

But there is no way that he is going to leave his flock without a shepherd. His solution is so beautiful:

> *For this is what the Sovereign LORD says: I myself will search for my sheep and look after them. As a shepherd looks after his scattered flock when he is with them, so will I look after my sheep. I will rescue them from all the places where they were scattered on a day of clouds and darkness. (v 11-12)*

God promised that he would come in person and take personal responsibility for shepherding the sheep. And he did! When Jesus looked at the religious leaders of his day and saw them crushing the sheep, he declared, "I am the good shepherd" (John 10:11). The Sovereign Lord has come, and now the sheep are gloriously safe.

Jesus is the Shepherd who comes to lead us where we have a tendency to get lost. Jesus says, "Follow me"—that is shepherd language. We so often think that we know what we should do and how we should live. We come to Jesus and say, "Please help me to do all this stuff that I have decided is definitely what I want to do". That is not following. Rather, we must adopt the posture of a sheep and ask that he might lead us. We must listen to what he says in his word and do it. It might sometimes feel hard, but our Shepherd knows what he is doing. Freedom is not found in going our own way. It is found in following his way.

Jesus comes to feed us. We live in a hungry world where people are desperately looking for satisfaction. We can stuff ourselves so full of distractions and rubbish that we have no space to rest and find satisfaction in Jesus. Jesus is your Shepherd who alone can satisfy your deepest hunger. He will provide for you and care for you. He doesn't promise that everything will be easy, but he does promise to walk with you. He will feed you with all that you need so that you can live a full life into eternity.

And Jesus is the Shepherd who protects us. When a lion is attacking the sheep, a good shepherd stands between his sheep and the danger. That is Jesus. Supremely at the cross, Jesus stood between us and the great enemy of death that we deserve. He stretched out his arms and protected us. The full force of death fell on him so that we might be shielded. There will be difficult days when the darkness threatens us. But even in that darkest of valleys, Jesus is with us to protect us and lead us safely home.

Jesus is wonderful because he is the Sovereign Lord come in person to shepherd his sheep. In him you will find one who leads you, feeds you and will protect you for ever.

Which aspect of Jesus' shepherding do you feel most in need of today? Come to him. You could read Psalm 23 slowly and enjoy the reality of Jesus as your Shepherd.

18

The Glory

We have seen his glory.

John 1:14

We are on a search for glory. People travel the world to see sights that dazzle. People gaze at the stars and point telescopes into the vast depths of space. People gather in crowds to witness beautiful art that transports the soul to another dimension. All of it is an ache for glory. We long to experience something that evokes wonder within us.

That happened to Isaiah in the most spectacular way. He saw God high and exalted and sitting on his throne. We can't begin to imagine it. It is a bit like standing at the bottom of the Grand Canyon and being overwhelmed by the size and majesty—but so much more. He *saw* God. The only detail he really managed to comprehend was the very edge of God's robe that filled the whole temple. That alone was enough. Angelic beings circled around, the air was filled with the noise of their voices saying, "Holy, holy, holy is the Lord Almighty" (Isaiah 6:3). Smoke poured out and the earth shook. It completely consumed Isaiah—he wasn't looking at his watch and wondering what was for dinner. It was an awe-inspiring, heart-exposing, time-pausing, earth-shattering experience.

But here is the critical question: what was it that Isaiah actually saw?

John's Gospel tells us that Isaiah "saw Jesus' glory and spoke about him" (John 12:41). Isaiah saw the glory of Jesus. That is really big. This should stretch our view of Jesus beyond the man bound by his earthly life. Before Mary saw him as a baby, Isaiah saw him in all his glory.

If this is true, then it means that Isaiah's experience in the temple was not a one-off event that was just for him. It is what all of us can experience when we look at Jesus. As John writes his Gospel, he is absolutely convinced that all of us can see the glory of God when we come and meet Jesus in his word.

Let me unpack three aspects of glory that might help us to engage with Jesus more. Firstly, it is a *visible* thing. God is unseen; he is invisible, and yet he is not hiding from us. He reveals his glory in visible ways so that we might know him. He has revealed his glory in creation, which is why we taste the transcendent when we see a beautiful sunrise. He reveals himself in great acts of history. But most supremely, he reveals his glory in his Son. Jesus is the invisible God made visible. Jesus is the glory of God—and that is what Isaiah saw. We are not to settle for a purely intellectual understanding of the Bible. Rather we should read with a hungry desire that we might see more of the glory of Christ. Have we lost our expectation to see more of him?

Secondly, glory is a *weighty* thing. It is serious, not trivial. Isaiah was not entertained by the glory of God; he was awe-struck by it. A generation that has grown up in a materialistic world has a very shrivelled capacity for awe. So perhaps we find that reading the Bible feels like hard work. It might appear to be slow moving compared to the latest Netflix series. But if we will gaze on Christ, we will engage with the weightiest and deepest truths of the universe. This won't happen in a snatched five minutes as we dash out of the door. It won't happen in distracted scrolling through our phone. We need to recapture a hunger for glory and the relentless pursuit of something that lasts. Jesus is not a nice man who said some interesting things. He is the ultimate reality, the weight that holds the whole universe in place.

Thirdly, glory is a *transforming* thing. If you encounter the glory of God, you will never be the same. Isaiah was completely broken by what he saw. He felt exposed—his own sin was suddenly crystal clear to him. "Woe to me … I am a man of unclean lips" (Isaiah 6:5). It wasn't a nice experience that left him feeling warm and fuzzy. It was a powerful experience that left him deeply conscious of his need for God's grace and love. And the love of God met him in that place, forgave all his sin and gave his whole life new direction. That is what an encounter with the glory of Jesus will do for us too. We will find ourselves exposed and at the same time deeply loved. He meets us in our sin, forgives us and gives our lives a whole new direction.

Jesus is wonderful because he is the glory of God. He makes the unseen God visible so that we can know him. He is weighty and solid in a flimsy and fragile world. Encountering him will transform us as we realise our sinfulness and taste his stunning forgiveness.

How much do you hunger for a greater experience of the glory of God? You could ask God to open the eyes of your heart to see the glory of Jesus more and more.

19

The Redeemer

I know that my redeemer lives,
and that in the end he will stand on the earth.
And after my skin has been destroyed,
yet in my flesh I will see God;
I myself will see him
with my own eyes—I, and not another.

Job 19:25-27

Sometimes you get a glimpse of Jesus in the most unexpected places. That is certainly true in the Bible book of Job. Come and sit with Job for a few minutes and you might be surprised by what you find.

Job is an impressive individual by any standard. When we first meet him, he is living a life of blazing fullness: feasting and joy, family and community, wealth and honour. And behind it all was a deep love and respect for the God he worshipped. He is a model human being living in right relationship with God.

But there is a suspicion lurking in the background. Is this the real Job? What would happen if all he had was stripped away? Does Job *really* love God, or does he only love the good things God has given him? Has God bought Job's loyalty by showering him with blessings?

So, God puts his own reputation on the line and allows Job to undergo a great trial of his faith. Job loses everything: his wealth, his family, his health. He is overtaken by unimaginable suffering, and it leaves him completely broken. He is confused; he is tormented by questions and doubts; he sinks down to the lowest place. The blazing fire has been extinguished, and the former glory has gone. He is an empty shell who is bereft of everything.

Despite all that has been lost, one thing remains. If you lean in close, you will hear Job whisper it through his tears. "I know that my Redeemer lives" (Job 19:25).

It is all that Job has left but it is more than enough—Job still knows his Redeemer.

Job is not looking for the hero within himself—there isn't one. He is not summoning up extraordinary reserves of willpower and self-confidence—the tank is completely empty. No, Job is clinging to one final hope. There is someone who is stronger than him, who will stand when he has fallen. There is someone who has power when he has nothing. There is someone who can hold him even as life slips away. There is someone who can reach him when he is in the grave. There is someone who will raise him to new life with God. There is a Redeemer, and he is enough. Even in the face of death, he is enough.

Jesus is this great Redeemer that Job saw. In the darkest place, Jesus was enough for Job and he is enough for us too.

It is fairly easy to trust God when life is good and things are easy. But when all of that is stripped away, Jesus is enough.

Job didn't even know his name but we do. We have seen his power and compassion. He has come to us and entered our distress. He has experienced our weakness. He has faced death itself and three days later rose again to stand on the earth in victory.

When all else has crumbled away, Jesus will still stand. When death comes to our door and our lives slip away, he will hold us safe. We will be raised to new life, and we will see God—with new bodies, perfected eyes and transformed hearts.

Is Jesus your Redeemer today? Is he your hope? When all else is stripped away, when all power is gone, when darkness seems to be complete, will you defiantly whisper with Job, "I know that my Redeemer lives"?

He is enough.

Jesus is wonderful because he is our Redeemer who comes to us in our distress and lifts us up to stand with him and to see his face for ever.

How does the story of Job encourage you in the face of suffering?

20

The Passover Lamb

For Christ, our Passover lamb, has been sacrificed.

1 Corinthians 5:7

Every year, the people of God would stop and remember that day. Etched into their diaries and their memories was the great narrative that defined the collective identity of the nation of Israel. The essence of the story was very simple: once they had been slaves but now they were free. Once they had no identity but now they were the people of God. The enemy was defeated and now they could celebrate.

But the centrepiece of this annual festival seems very strange. It all revolved around a lamb. The central symbol was not a warrior, or an army, or a leader, but it was a lamb that represented their freedom. And it is all connected to our understanding of Jesus. Let's back up and see why.

The nation of Israel was enslaved by Pharaoh, the evil king (aka god) of Egypt. The people were groaning in deep distress. There seemed no hope of escape. But these were God's precious people; he was closely watching over them. He saw their misery and the time came for him to act. God was about to display his glory and set his people free. So he sent a man called Moses to deliver this message to Pharaoh:

> *This is what the LORD says: Israel is my firstborn son, and I told you, "Let my son go, so that he may worship me." But you refused to let him go; so I will kill your firstborn son. (Exodus 4:22-23)*

The battle lines were clearly drawn. The Exodus is a story of two firstborns. When Pharaoh threatened the firstborn son of God he made a very big mistake. It meant he was putting his own firstborn son at risk. Pharaoh set himself up against God.

The battle commenced and God sent nine plagues against all the false gods of Egypt. Each of them was terrible but not final. God was patiently warning Pharaoh of the disaster that was coming. But Pharaoh would not listen and so the conflict moved to the final stage.

There would be a clear division between the firstborn of God and the firstborn of Egypt. In every family, in every home, even among the animals, all the firstborn sons of Egypt would die. But every Israelite firstborn would be safe. In fact, they would be so safe that even a dog wouldn't bark at them (Exodus 11:7). This is the great judgment of God that spells the end of Egypt. God would protect his firstborn son and would devastate the enemy.

That all seemed very clear but then came the twist. God's people were told that their safety was not automatic. Now they were introduced to the central figure of the lamb.

In every home, a lamb was selected, and it lived with the family for four days (being treated like a son). On the night of judgment, it was sacrificed, and the blood was put on the doorframes. The lamb died instead of the firstborn son. The blood was put on the doorframe of the house as a sign that a death had occurred and so the judgment of God would pass over that home.

But why was all of that necessary? Surely God knew where the Egyptians lived. Why couldn't he just avoid the Israelite houses?

God was powerfully teaching his people that he did not love them because they are better than the Egyptians. They were not morally superior or intrinsically more valuable. Israel needed to know that they were not automatically immune from this judgment. He was providing the way for them to be safe, and it all happened through the lamb. Their freedom was bought at the cost of the sacrificed lamb.

But this festival to celebrate the Passover was not just pointing backwards to a past rescue. It was also pointing forward to a greater Lamb. When Jesus appears, the echoes of Passover are all over the place. Here is the beloved firstborn Son of God. Here is the one who is rightly identified as the Lamb of God. He comes and lives among us, identifies with us and becomes one of us. He is pure and perfect in every way. Jesus celebrates the Passover each year with (just imagine this) a growing awareness that this feast is actually all about him.

And then comes the great dramatic moment. The inescapable climax in each of the Gospel accounts is the Passover, but there is a breathtaking twist on the great old narrative. Rather than save his firstborn Son through the death of a lamb, instead God gives up his firstborn Son to *be* the Passover Lamb.

We can be rescued from the slavery of darkness and brought into freedom as God's children. But it does not happen because we are better than anyone else. He does not love you because you are morally superior. He loves you because he has provided the Lamb, who died as your substitute and now protects you from death for ever more.

Jesus is wonderful because he is our hero. He willingly offered himself in our place to purchase us for God. We now belong to God as his firstborn son. That is what the true Passover Lamb has done for us.

How does it feel to dwell on what you've been saved from? What will you do with the freedom that Jesus bought for you?

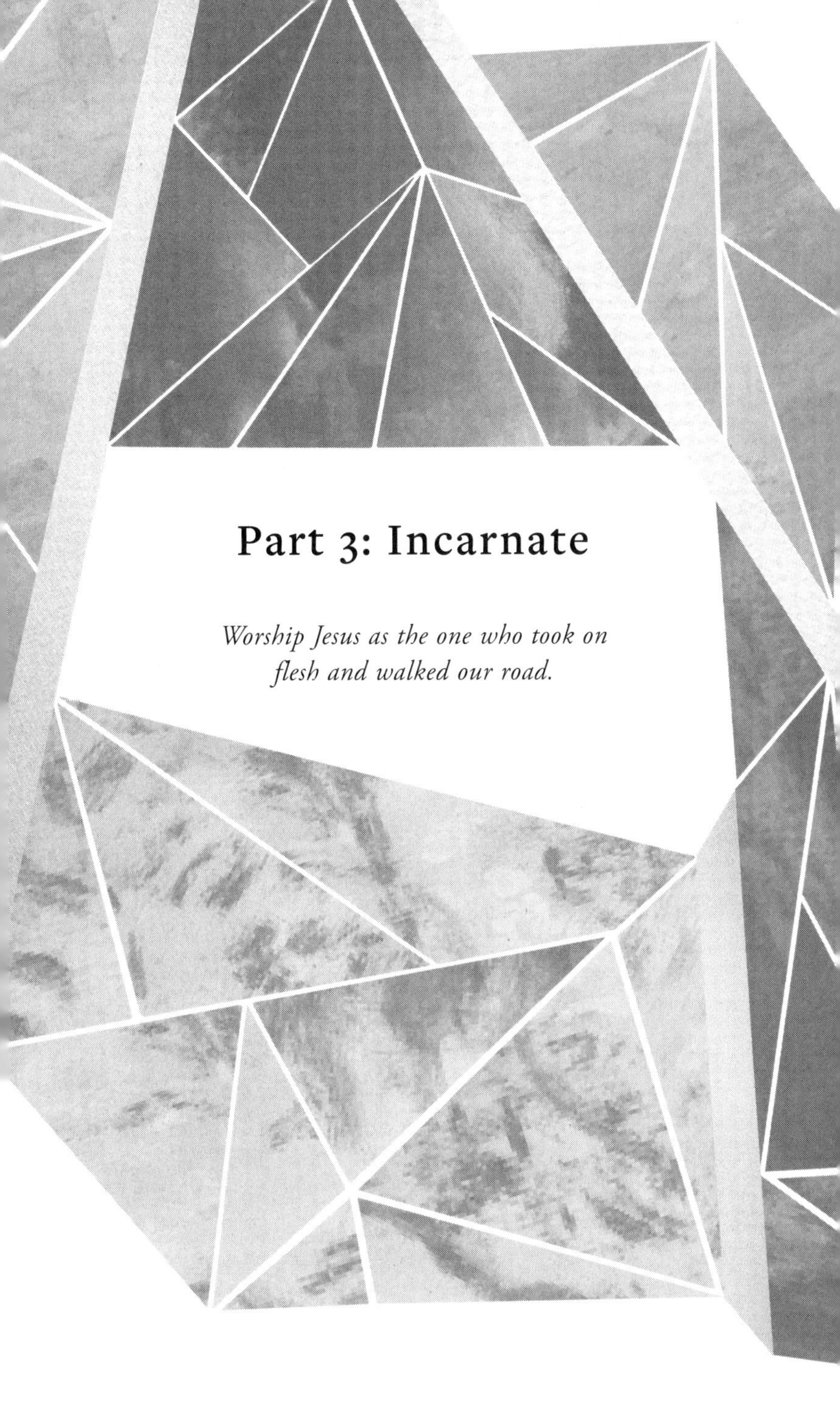

Part 3: Incarnate

Worship Jesus as the one who took on flesh and walked our road.

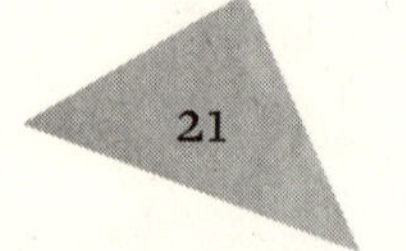

Made Flesh

The Word became flesh.

John 1:14

No other human philosophy or religion comes close to the reality contained in these four words: *the Word became flesh.*

Here it is in simple terms: God became human. The eternal Son of God had a birthday. The Word, who is the creative reality that lies behind the existence of all things, became a creature.

This is called the incarnation. Perhaps it might help us to understand better if we think of chilli-con-carne—it literally means chilli with meat. That is what the "carn" bit of incarnation is referring to. So we might (carefully) describe Jesus as "God con carne", that is, God with flesh.

It is such a daring claim that many have stumbled here. People have looked for a way to escape such a scandalous idea. Some have maintained that Jesus was not truly God—he was an ordinary man in whom God came to powerfully dwell by his Spirit. Others have argued that he only *seemed* to be human—he was fully God but never inhabited a truly human existence. But John is insistent that it was "the Word" himself who became flesh. Jesus gave up nothing of his deity. But in this willing act of love, he became what he had not been before. You can't escape it.

Two natures existed in the one person of Christ. A fully human nature and a fully divine nature. They existed in such a way that neither of the two natures was compromised or changed. He was both the Word, and he was flesh. He is rightly called God, and he is rightly called man.

Let's dwell here for a moment and let our imaginations feel the wonder. Picture the baby lying in the manger—the Creator of the stars now rests under a starry sky. The Sustainer of all things is now sustained by his mother's milk. He is three hours old, and he is the God who inhabits eternity. He is learning to talk and yet he is the God of eternal wisdom and knowledge.

We rightly marvel at the depths of this mystery.

The infinite God who fills the heavens is now contained within the limitations of a human body. The one who never slumbered nor slept (Psalm 121:4) is now the man who sleeps in a boat. The one who provides food for all living creatures (Psalm 145:16) now has a human stomach that aches with hunger. The immortal God who gives life to all things, now tastes the agonies and sorrow of death. This is what God chose to do.

This dignifies our human bodily existence in a remarkable way. Any idea that God is only interested in our souls is blown out of the water. We can quickly get frustrated with the limitations of our bodies and are disappointed by the mundane realities of life. We might see our bodies as a prison that we need to escape from.

That is a serious misunderstanding. Jesus dignifies an embodied existence. He lived the commonplace life of a carpenter. He grew up in an ordinary town. He walked ordinary streets. And all that while being the eternal Son of God. To be an ordinary human is a great honour; our bodies are fearfully and wonderfully made. When Jesus was knit together in his mother's womb, he revealed that it is a very good thing to have a body.

But our bodies are also decaying. They are weak and frail. Human sin has brought death to our world. We ache, we groan, we hunger, we die. It is as though we are drowning in a stormy ocean and cannot swim. Jesus is not like the lifeguard who shouts instructions to swim. He does not throw out a rope in the hope of dragging us to safety. He leaves the security of his boat and lunges himself into our reality. He became weak and frail flesh in order that he might take hold of us and lift us to safety.

Our bodies are beautiful, and they are broken. So, Jesus was made flesh in order that he might both dignify and redeem our bodies for ever.

Jesus is wonderful because he willingly and completely entered the raging waters of our sin in order to save us, body and soul, and restore us to God our Father.

What most amazes you about the fact that God became human?

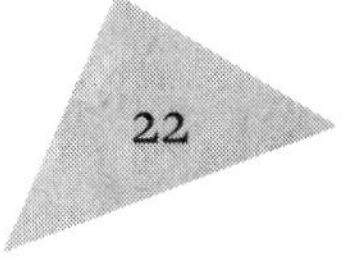

Like Us

For what the law was powerless to do because it was weakened by the flesh, God did by sending his own Son in the likeness of sinful flesh.

Romans 8:3

The Son of God became like us. That sounds comforting and wonderful but what does it really mean? After all, we experience powerful internal desires for things that we know are wrong. Did Jesus? We often get to the end of a day and feel frustrated or disappointed at the ways we have behaved. Did Jesus? We find that sin is irresistible to us—we feel enslaved and wish we could change. Did Jesus?

These are critical questions that begin to make us wonder whether Jesus wasn't really like us at all. Was he really tempted or was he just pretending? Did he really struggle or was it just an act? Perhaps he was like a mime artist who creates the illusion of carrying a heavy load when there is actually nothing there at all. If Jesus didn't sin, then how can he be like us?

Two Bible truths might help us make progress.

1. Sin is not intrinsic to being human

We were not originally created with sinful desires and internal battles. For a brief moment, our first parents lived a beautiful life untainted by sin. All their desires were good and rightly ordered towards the good things that God created. But then the external temptation of the serpent distorted and subverted their internal desires in such a way that, for the first time, humanity desired what God had forbidden. They chose to follow that misdirected desire and from that point on they became enslaved to sin. This is what the Bible means when it talks about the sinful nature. Every baby since then has been born into that same condition of slavery to sin.

But being born with a fallen sinful nature is not the essence of what it means to be truly human. In fact, you could argue that to be free from this slavery is to be more fully human than the fallen existence we experience. When Jesus became like us, it does not mean that he inherited a sinful nature.

2. Jesus did live in a sinful world

Although Jesus did not have a fallen nature, he did live in a fallen world. He was not in the same position as Adam who lived out his pre-sin existence in a very good garden. Jesus entered our world that is ravaged by the devastating impact of human sin. He had a body like ours that fully suffered the effects of the curse that sin had unleashed. Paul says that Jesus was made "in the likeness of sinful flesh" (Romans 8:3). Wow. That is a very carefully constructed sentence. Jesus did not just become "flesh" but entered into the reality of "sinful flesh". That means he lived in this world of decay and frustration, sorrow and pain. And he experienced those realities fully. He had a human body that was decaying.

But Paul is careful to make clear that there was an important difference. His humanity was not identical to ours. He came in the *likeness* of sinful flesh. He became *as much like us as is possible* without his internal self being polluted by sinful desire. He did not fail where Adam failed. His desires were always rightly ordered towards all that is good. He faced the same serpent but the external temptation never disrupted or distorted his internal desires. He lived the maximal human life in the face of extreme pressure to cave in.

This means that Jesus really did become like us. He walked our road of suffering. He experienced the frustration of a world where things go wrong, and wood splits, and accidents happen, and people get sick, and friends die, and people betray you. He became like us in all those ways, which means he understands us. But he also became like us in the sense of what we should have been. He lived the life we were created to live. He lived a more human life than we have ever experienced. You could say that he is more like us than we are!

And this is what qualifies him to be the Saviour. He had to be like us in order to fully represent us as our Priest. He had to be like us in order to step in for us as our substitute.

He had to be like us in order to redeem our whole human existence, both body and soul, and restore us to God. He is the new Adam who reverses the devastating curse that our first parents brought into the world. Jesus became like us, so that we could become like him.

Jesus is wonderful because he became like us yet was not tainted by sin. He became like us, so he understands us. He became like us so that he could save us.

Why is it such good news that Jesus is like us but did not sin? How does that encourage you to become more like him?

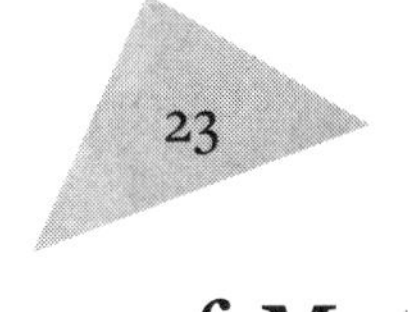

Son of Man

In my vision at night I looked, and there before me was one like a son of man.

Daniel 7:13

We like simple answers; we like things to be clear. But many things in life are a puzzle that draw us into more careful thought.

When Jesus called himself the Son of Man it was an invitation into a puzzle. He could have chosen the much more obvious title of Messiah or King or Son of God. But instead, he preferred the enigmatic name, Son of Man. It makes you wonder why…

It fits with a pattern in Jesus' teaching where he spoke in ways that left people puzzled and scratching their heads. This wasn't Jesus being deliberately awkward, but he did want to make people think. He knows the human tendency to make assumptions and to jump to quick conclusions. He wanted people to slow down, listen carefully, think deeply, watch closely and learn what he was truly saying.

The title "Son of Man" is an invitation to do just that—to set aside our own expectations and let Jesus teach us. Here are some thoughts to get you started, but the more we slow down and listen to Jesus, the more riches we will find in this beautiful name.

The Son of Man is a name with layers of meaning. On the surface level, it simply means human. The Hebrew phrase is *ben* (son of) *adam* (man—meaning the ground from where we came). It reminds human beings of our humble beginnings, our human limitations and our common destiny of death. We are all sons and daughters of Adam. We all came from dust.

Jesus calling himself the Son of Man is, in some ways, an unremarkable thing. He is identifying himself as a true human being with a body that is made from the dust of the earth. This is why people don't seem to take much notice of this name. It is very ordinary.

But Adam was more than just a creature moulded together from a lump of clay. He was also entrusted with the extraordinary privilege of being the image of God in the world. Human beings were created to represent God in his creation. It was a great honour—but Adam trashed it.

So, when Jesus comes, calling himself the Son of Man, he is identifying himself as the true human who will be the perfect image of God. Jesus is the man that Adam failed to be. Jesus is humanity as we were meant to be.

But that isn't it for this title. Jesus uses it in specific ways that push us to search deeper. Here are the references in Mark's Gospel: Jesus is the Son of Man (human being) who has the authority to forgive sins (Mark 2:10); he is the Lord of the Sabbath (2:28); he is the one who is going to suffer and die (8:31) and he will do that in order to give his life as a ransom for others (10:45).

These statements are a conundrum. A human being who can forgive sin. An authority figure who will suffer. The Lord who will give his life.

Then, in Mark 14, it all comes out. Jesus is on trial before the religious leaders and they are desperate to find a way to execute him. Finally, they ask him, "Are you the Messiah, the Son of the Blessed One?" (v 61). Jesus answers, "I am … And you will see the Son of Man sitting at the right hand of the Mighty One and coming on the clouds of heaven" (v 62).

With that, Jesus seals his fate. By this point, it is clear that Son of Man means something much, much bigger than simply being human. He is evoking a powerful passage from the prophet Daniel. Daniel saw a vision of the throne room of heaven and sitting on the throne was the Ancient of Days. Clearly this is God who alone is worthy of worship. Then another character enters the scene—one "like a son of man" (Daniel 7:13). He appears to be human, but he is led right into God's presence and then (and this will blow away all our categories) this human figure is given "authority, glory and sovereign power". Daniel is also shown that "all nations and peoples of every language worshipped him. His dominion is an everlasting dominion that will not pass away, and his kingdom is one that will never be destroyed" (v 14).

This is no mere man. This is the human yet divine figure who becomes the object of heaven's worship. Jesus is claiming that he is that figure.

Here is where we start to solve the puzzle. Jesus is both spectacularly ordinary and also the one who is the object of heaven's worship. No wonder people couldn't understand him. No wonder we struggle to wrap our minds around who he is. But isn't he magnificent?

Jesus is wonderful because he is the Son of Man. He is so very ordinary and yet will be the object of our eternal worship.

How does this description of Jesus stretch your mind and draw you more deeply to worship?

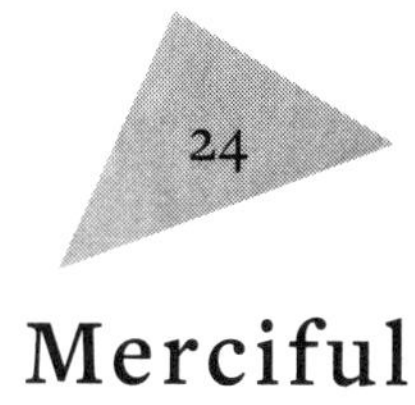

Merciful

Jesus, Son of David, have mercy on me!

Mark 10:47

How do you feel when you are interrupted? You have made your important plans for the day—and then the doorbell rings.

It seems to me that the more "important" you become, the greater the desire for interruptions to be eliminated. Sometimes barriers line the streets so that the important people don't get interrupted by the normal people. They can stare but not come too close. At other times, police escorts whizz along the streets clearing the ordinary cars out of the way so that the chosen celebrity can carry on their day without being disrupted. The message is painfully clear: important people are busy and should not be disturbed.

I think this is why some of us pride ourselves on being busy. It gives us a sense of importance and worth. But the reality is that, as our lives get busier, our capacity for mercy is diminished. Perhaps busyness is a really poor indicator of importance.

What about Jesus? There is no one with greater worth and importance. The eternal Son of God became a man to go to a cross to save the world. No one had a more significant role or a more important to-do list. Yet in Mark 10:49 we read my two favourite words in the whole of Mark's Gospel:

Jesus stopped.

As he walked along the road with his face set towards Jerusalem and his imminent death, Jesus saw something that made him stop and put his own plans on hold. What could be so significant that Jesus would allow such an interruption to the divine agenda?

The answer should turn our world upside down. It wasn't a king or an influencer. It wasn't someone with nobility or celebrity but a blind beggar called Bartimaeus. He was sitting there and shouting out, "Jesus, Son of David, have mercy on me!" (v 38).

The crowd clearly don't think he is worthy to receive a slice of Jesus' precious time. They tell him to stop shouting—Jesus is far too busy for someone so unimportant. He is at the back of the queue and needs to remember his place. Stay behind the barrier and keep quiet.

But still, he keeps on shouting. His urgent cries reveal that he sees (ironically) more than anyone else can see. He knows that Jesus is the Messianic Son of David. He sees that Jesus is the King of God's kingdom who maybe, just maybe, might be willing to stop and show him mercy.

What other hope has he got?

The crowd don't see it, but this blind man has got it exactly right. And Jesus stopped. To stop for someone in desperate need is the very definition of mercy. Jesus is not the busy king, he is the merciful King.

And there is more. Jesus does not simply waft his hand over the man and heal him as he sweeps by. He treats the man with wonderful dignity. He does not assume that he knows what the man wants, but he calls for the man to come to him and asks, "What do you want me to do for you?" (v 51).

Jesus takes the time to hear the man's story. He wants to understand the deep longing of this broken man's heart. And so, the man pours out years of pain and heartache in his simple request, "Rabbi, I want to see" (v 51). Jesus is moved with mercy towards this man and heals him. Bartimaeus is transformed by mercy.

This is the beautiful heart of our King Jesus. He comes near to the broken-hearted and stops to show mercy. When we cry out to him from the depths of our need, he stops to hear us. He comes near to us too; he is not too busy to hear your cry.

I also find that this story challenges my busy heart. Do we stop and see the needs all around us or do we rush around, too busy with our own agenda to let people interrupt and change our plans for the day?

Jesus is wonderful because he stops to show mercy to anyone who asks him.

Do you ever feel like Jesus is too busy to be interested in your need? How does the mercy of Jesus challenge us in our busy lives?

Gentle

I am gentle and humble in heart.

Matthew 11:29

As a species, we have a very high capacity for irritation. Tourists walking slowly, people driving badly, children demanding loudly, toothpaste squeezed wrongly, sports stars performing poorly, colleagues thinking differently… All of these scenarios have the potential to cause an eruption of harsh thinking and words. It can happen so quickly. And if we are tired or hungry it only seems to be worse.

Jesus is wonderful because he was never harsh. Isn't that remarkable? When he was tired, he was gentle. Even when he was pushed to the very limit, he remained kind. When his disciples were slow to understand, rather than storm off in anger, he continued to love them. When his enemies came to arrest him, he could have unleashed all the armies of heaven, but he allowed himself to be led meekly away.

When they hurled their insults at him, he could have rained down fire from the sky, but he prayed that they might be forgiven. Even when he was speaking hard truth, he was never harsh.

We need to dig deeper to see the true source of that gentleness.

Our harsh words are normally a symptom of a deeper problem in the heart. Although we would never put it this way, we begin to think that the people around us exist for our own convenience. Rather than seeing them as precious image-bearers of God, subconsciously they become either assets or obstacles to my enjoyment of life. My agenda and my desires take centre stage, and I expect others to get in line (or at least not get in the way).

When someone helps our lives run smoothly then the harsh heart is not very evident. We think nice thoughts and we say kind and encouraging words. But don't be fooled—that is not gentleness, that is flattery. We simply want them to keep acting that way because it is good for us.

The challenge comes when people become an inconvenience. When they become a burden, when they make demands of us—and it starts to get costly. Then the harsh heart can kick into gear, and we unleash our frustrations. We become critical, judgemental, sulky and irritable. We instinctively react with harsh words that can unleash great damage. But all of that starts in the heart.

This is the key to the gentleness of Jesus: his heart was always oriented towards loving others. Rather than crushing us with expectation, he comes alongside us to lift the burdens from our shoulders. Rather than demanding that people that serve him, instead he came to first serve us. Rather than seeing us as assets to be used, he sees us children to be loved.

We can sometimes assume that being gentle is about being weak or soft or quiet. It could not be more different—it is the act of the will to use my strength and my resources to do others good rather than harm. When you put it like that, the stronger you are, the greater your capacity for gentleness.

If I get in a boxing ring with the heavyweight champion of the world and I say, "Please be gentle with me", I am not suggesting that he is weak. Instead, I am recognising that he has the power to completely flatten me, and I am asking him to hold back that power in order to do me good.

That is gentleness. Jesus has all the power of God at his disposal, yet he chooses not to use that power for his own comfort and ease. His heart is entirely taken up with the people that he came to serve. He uses his enormous might to carry our burdens and to save us. He uses his great strength to come alongside us and to help us. Never to crush, never to mock, never to be harsh—only to love and to do good.

Jesus is wonderful because he is utterly gentle towards his people. In our weakness and foolishness, Jesus chooses to use all his power to heal and restore us.

Where do you need to experience the gentleness of Jesus? Where do you find yourself challenged to be gentle towards others?

26 Self-Controlled

He was hungry.

Luke 4:2

"No" is a fascinating little word. It can be cruel and harsh, but it can also be loving and life-giving. It can be restrictive but it can also be liberating. It can be the hardest word to say, and it can be the easiest. Learning to use it rightly is the pursuit of a lifetime.

Most importantly, each of us needs to learn how to use it when it comes to our own heart's desires.

We each have a complex web of appetites and desires. Many of them are directed towards fundamentally good things. But the problem is that they need to be controlled, because the human heart has a terrible habit of going rogue. Good desires that are left unchecked become controlling desires that can end up enslaving us—and then we are in serious trouble. Here is the reality: if you don't learn to control your desires in a way which is healthy and good, you will quickly find that your desires are controlling you and leading you to places that are dark and dangerous.

But Jesus is different. He is beautiful because he perfectly displayed the art of saying no to his own desires before they could ever take root as controlling desires. He shows us that self-control is being able to say *no* to our desires in order to pursue something greater.

There was a time when he spent 40 days in the desert and ate nothing. Luke 4:2 says that "at the end of them he was hungry". Unsurprisingly, he experienced a strong heart desire for food. Yet when he was tempted to use his own power to serve that desire, he said no. He refused to let his good desire for food control his behaviour. He rejected self-reliance and chose faithful obedience.

But there were plenty of other times when Jesus ate good food with friends and enjoyed a party. He always knew when to say yes to his desires and when to say no. He experienced all sorts of desires just like we do—there is nothing sinful in that. But every time a desire of his heart arose within him, he always answered it rightly. He said yes when it would honour his Father and no when it would do harm.

Think of this: it means that Jesus never regretted anything that he did. He feasted but never regretted indulging. He rested but never regretted wasting a morning in bed. He enjoyed deep friendships but was never controlled by sexual desires.

How often have we let the desires of our hearts control us? How often have we put up no fight and simply said yes? How often have we experienced that painful moment of regret? Jesus never got it wrong and this is what makes him wonderful.

And then, perhaps most poignantly of all, think of him in the Garden of Gethsemane. He experiences the desire to avoid death. He desires to avoid pain. He recoils from the agony that he is about to suffer. You can hear it in the anguished prayer that he prayed, "Take this cup from me" (Luke 22:42).

Those are good desires, but Jesus does not allow them to control his decisions. He perfectly and masterfully puts those desires in their rightful place as he prays, "Yet not what I will, but what you will" (Mark 14:36).

Jesus says no to the powerful desires surging through his mind as he chose to say yes to the perfect will of God. The Bible book of Hebrews expresses a similar idea in this striking sentence:

> *For the joy that was set before him he endured the cross, scorning its shame, and sat down at the right hand of the throne of God. (Hebrews 12:2)*

Jesus said no to self in order to say yes to saving us. Praise God for his perfect self-control.

Jesus is wonderful because he was never controlled by his desires like we are. He learned to say no at the right times and he can teach us to do the same.

Where do you find that your desires begin to take control of you? Ask Jesus to help you grow in the beautiful fruit of self-control.

Atonement

Take this cup from me.

Mark 14:36

The perfect stillness of the garden is punctured by the haunting noise of a man crying out in distress. It is a sound that gives a glimpse into the most profound moment of human agony.

Jesus kneels to plead with his Father. He has one desperate request: "Take this cup from me". This is the thing that fills Jesus with overwhelming sorrow as he contemplates all that he is about to face. It isn't the betrayal, or the cruelty, or the mockery, or the nails, or the nakedness, or the rejection or even the death. It is drinking this cup that will bring upon Jesus the greatest horror of all.

In the face of such suffering he could easily have slipped away into the shadows of the garden and saved himself. Yet he prayed. And he stayed. And he obeyed. Why?

He was driven by a deeper love that understood there was no other way to save humanity.

We need to understand why the cup brought such anguish upon Jesus. It is an Old Testament symbol that represents the greatest threat that has ever engulfed our world. The prophet Jeremiah was told by God:

> *Take from my hand this cup filled with the wine of my wrath and make all the nations to whom I send you drink it. (Jeremiah 25:15)*

This cup is filled with the wine of God's wrath. This is God's right response to human unfaithfulness. It is the cup of exile, the cup of destruction, the cup of punishment. Swallowing it means to be shut out of God's presence. Jesus knows he must drink it—no wonder he shuddered at the thought.

We might find it hard to hear of God's wrath. Instinctively we prefer to think of God as love. Yet it is a mistake to set these two things against one another as if they were opposites. Deep, passionate, consistent love will always overflow in controlled and right opposition to anything that threatens that love. That is what real love does, isn't it?

God loves this world too much to turn a blind eye to wickedness and injustice. He will not pretend that our sin against him and against one another does not matter. It does. It destroys everything. Perfect love will always oppose and act against such a destructive reality. And so again and again God warns rebellious people of this coming cup.

But it is a warning, not a threat. This warning is designed to stop people in their tracks, calling them to turn back to him. Like Jonah preaching to the wicked city of Nineveh in the Old Testament, the very warning of judgment contains the promise that disaster can be averted.

The cup of God's wrath was coming to Nineveh. They were about to destroyed, but when they heard the warning, they repented. They cried out for mercy and God forgave all their wickedness. Essentially, they asked God to *take the cup away from them* and immediately he said *yes*.

But what about all their sin? What happens to the cup? Does it simply evaporate into thin air, and we just pretend it never existed? Come to think of it, what about an adulterer like King David or a murderer like Moses or a liar like Jacob? How can they all be forgiven? How can the cup of God's wrath be removed from them?

There is a problem here. How can God forgive sinners but also punish wickedness? Who will drink the cup of God's wrath if it is taken away from those who deserve to drink it? These are all questions of atonement. Sin has been left unpunished. How can that be?

Come back to the garden and see the man praying. He will drink the cup that sinners deserve. He will face the punishment that Jacob, Moses, David, the Ninevites and countless millions more deserve. He will make atonement as he drains the cup of the horrifying judgment of God.

This is not an innocent third party or a random stranger but the eternal Son of God. He who had never sinned would now become sin for us. He who was the eternal object of his Father's joy and delight would now become an object of wrath. He who was the author of life would be handed over to death until the cup was fully drained and now not a drop remains for us.

Full atonement. Loving forgiveness. Beautiful justice.

Jesus is wonderful because he willingly drank the cup that brings us complete atonement. There is no more punishment for us to face.

Where might you be in danger of taking the work of Jesus for granted?

Sin Bearing

"He himself bore our sins" in his body on the cross.

1 Peter 2:24

For 18 years she had been unable to stand up straight. She was bent over and could only look at the floor. She shuffled into the synagogue each week and then shuffled home. Eyes down. Unable to join with the joyful praise of the people. Can you picture her?

This woman's physical condition is a powerful image of a spiritual condition that many people experience: a crushing weight of failure that holds us in the grip of shame. We cannot lift our heads in joyful worship because guilt keeps us bent over. We come to church, we see other people joyfully singing and we just feel empty. Perhaps we try and smile but deep inside we feel ashamed. We might know in theory that we are forgiven but we are yet to experience the full freedom of knowing that our sin has been completely taken away.

It is like receiving an invitation to share in an exquisite banquet. The bill has been paid, and I am welcomed to sit and eat freely in the beautiful dining room. But as I enter the feast, I realise that I am dressed in filthy clothes. As I take my seat, I am painfully aware that I'm not worthy. The feast is amazing, but I am not rejoicing. My head is bowed and I feel ashamed. My eyes are on the floor.

Here is the mixed-up reality that we often experience. We know that Jesus has paid for our sin. We know that we are welcomed to the great banquet that he has prepared. But we still feel filthy and unworthy. We feel like imposters and find it hard to truly rejoice.

That is not where Jesus leaves us. When Jesus met that woman, he performed an amazing miracle. Luke records the impact on that woman's life:

Immediately she straightened up and praised God.
(Luke 13:13)

The freedom Jesus brings is a back-straightening, chin-lifting, smile-bringing, head-raising, praise-releasing freedom. Jesus does not save us just so that we can shuffle around with our gaze on the ground. Salvation is so much more than that.

He not only paid the punishment our sin deserves but he also carried our sin upon his shoulders and removed it from us. It is this double work that leaves us not just legally right with God but also relationally right with him. He saves us from wrath, and he also sets us free from shame. This is why the sin-bearing work of Jesus is so crucial to our joy.

"He himself bore our sins" in his body on the cross.
(1 Peter 2:24)

As Jesus died, the heavy weight of our sin was lifted from us, and it crushed him. His head was bowed low, and his body was bent over. Because he took it on himself, now anyone who comes to him can experience that liberation.

God is not ignoring your sin. He is not pretending that your sin doesn't exist and he's not just tolerating it. He has removed it. We know that is true because the Bible declares it to be so:

> *As far as the east is from the west,*
> *so far has he removed our transgressions from us.*
> *(Psalm 103:12)*

> *Your guilt is taken away and your sin atoned for.*
> *(Isaiah 6:7)*

Lift up your head and take this in: our sins are gone. They do not need to continue to hang over us and accuse us. They are not stored up in a book somewhere ready to be dumped on us the next time we step out of line. Forgiveness means that our sin is completely removed. And not just your past sins but your future ones too. Every day we fail. Every day we sin. And every day we can come and confess those sins and know that they have been taken away because Jesus bore them on the cross.

Do you feel your back beginning to straighten? Will you raise your eyes to heaven in joyful praise?

Jesus is wonderful because he carried the weight of all of our sin. We are free to have an unburdened relationship with him.

Where do you feel like an unworthy imposter? How does this story encourage you today?

Victorious

... triumphing over them by the cross.

Colossians 2:15

Not all guilt is bad. It can drive us to a deeper love and dependence on Jesus. But there is a bad sort of guilt that eats away at us and keeps us enslaved. We feel a constant sense of our unworthiness and shame. Our joy is robbed, and our spiritual progress is stopped in its tracks. Where does that enslaving guilt come from?

The Bible is clear that Satan is the accuser, and bad guilt comes from him. He deploys this weapon over and over again in the minds of God's precious daughters and sons. Like the venom of a viper or the claws of a bear, Satan lashes out with poisonous allegations that tear into our hearts.

He never takes a break from his relentless assault on our consciences. He accuses God's people day and night (Revelation 12:10). He is the finger pointer. The gleeful prosecutor. The skilful litigator. He loves it when people sin because it loads his guns with more ammunition to aim straight back at us.

Here is the treachery of this enemy—he goes to great lengths to persuade us to sin and then when we finally snap, he turns on us with vicious accusations. How many people have been caught in his web of guilt and shame? How many people are held captive by their deep and profound sense of failure? How many people feel the demonic finger of blame pointing right at their hearts?

This is the greatest weapon Satan has against us. And, let's face it, he doesn't exactly have to make things up; human sin gives him a lot of material to work with. His accusations are true and expose our failure. We all have things that cause us to feel guilty. Satan loves to weaponise our shame to cause havoc in our hearts. Many of us feel it as a daily reality.

This is why we need to hear the glorious truth of Colossians 2:15—the Lord Jesus has disarmed Satan. He has de-fanged the serpent. He has silenced the bully. He has robbed the accuser of his most powerful weapon. At the cross, Jesus died so that no accusation that Satan brings can ever stand against you. Satan has no ammunition left and you are free.

In Colossians 2:14, Paul uses four powerful images to help us understand that Satan's accusations no longer have any teeth. Enjoy these words and let them wash your guilty conscience clean:

- Through the cross, God *forgave* us all our sins. God does not hold any of our sin against us. All of it, every part, has been forgiven. How can that be?

- It is only possible because the legal charge that stood against us has been *cancelled*. The solution to a guilty conscience is not to ignore sin or pretend it doesn't matter. Sin is deadly serious. Our lives rack up a devastating list of charges against us. There is an un-payable debt that stands as a constant voice of condemnation, but it has been cancelled. Not put on hold. Not postponed. Not suspended. But cancelled. What a beautiful word that is. How can that be?

- Our sin has been *taken away* from us. It has been lifted from our shoulders and removed from our account. What once declared our guilt has now been taken away. Do you feel the relief? Can you picture the great debt that would have overwhelmed you but has been lifted from your shoulders? How can that be?

- It has been *nailed* to the cross. The charge sheet that condemned me now has a massive hole ripped through it by a brutal Roman nail. It has been paid in full. The debt I owe and the condemnation I deserve were all pinned on Jesus and he willingly paid it all.

The cross of Jesus has completely disarmed Satan and left him powerless. He will still try to point the finger but there is no more power in his accusations. The victory is complete—we are not guilty anymore.

Jesus is wonderful because he has disarmed Satan and set me free from guilt and shame.

How do these images help you silence the enemy when he comes with his accusations against you?

Servant

Even the Son of Man did not come
to be served but to serve.

Mark 10:45

The British are world-renowned for their ability to queue. We will quietly stand in line for hours, but don't be fooled into thinking that we are happy. The queue actually creates great anxiety and stress. There is serious angst when we realise that we have chosen the slowest line. There is disgust with anyone who gains an unfair advantage and jumps ahead. If you scratch the surface, you will quickly discover that what appears to be a polite row of people is actually a group of individuals seething with suspicion and sharp elbows (without breaking the queueing rules of course).

To put it bluntly, we all want to be at the front. We want to make progress. We want to push forward. There is something of that desire within every human being. It's the same issue in so many areas of life: traffic jams, career progression, salary increases, holiday opportunities, achievements of our children and so on—we want to get ahead of those around us.

That same desire burned in the hearts of Jesus' disciples. We see this in what took place on the night before Jesus died. It is hard to imagine a more poignant moment—the taste of the bread and wine was still in their mouths. And then this happened:

> *A dispute also arose among them as to which of them was considered to be greatest. (Luke 22:24)*

How could this conversation possibly have happened at *that* table? It seems impossible. And yet it is also so very, very obvious. The natural human heart jostles for position; it looks for any advantage to push ahead; it hates the thought that it might miss out. Even in the most significant moments of life, it rushes forward to seek to establish itself at the front of the queue.

It is deeply unattractive.

Imagine the pain in Jesus' heart as he listens to the conversation. Have they learnt nothing from their years with him? So, once again, Jesus patiently sets about the task of redefining greatness. He asks a simple question: *At an extravagant banquet who are the "great" ones? The waiters bringing the food, or the guests being served?* The answer is obvious: everyone wants to be among the sitters not the servers. But then comes the hammer blow from Jesus:

> *I am among you as one who serves. (v 27)*

The central reality of Jesus' mission was to serve—serving wasn't a nice thing he sometimes did alongside his other more important work. It *was* his work. That is monumental. The eternal Son of God, the Creator, entered our world in order that he might serve us. It literally cost him everything and yet he willingly poured out his life. In every possible sense, Jesus went to the back of the queue and made himself last.

In our world, lesser people serve the greater ones. But not in the kingdom of God. Here you find that the greater serve the lesser. That is the life Jesus lived and the greatness that he defines. This feels profoundly uncomfortable to our naturally proud hearts. It seems so counterintuitive. But Jesus is insistent on this point. In every moment of his life he demonstrated this dynamic, and he says that it's the way into his kingdom.

So here is the deal: we need to learn to go to the back of the queue and serve others. To let others go ahead of us. To encourage others forward. To desire that others would be noticed and seen instead of ourselves. The back of the queue is where you find Jesus. The back of the queue is where you find the ones Jesus loves to serve.

And here is the secret that no one ever tells you about the back of the queue: this is where truest freedom is found. Pushing your way forward will lead to a lifetime of stress, disappointment, broken relationships and pain (think of the angst in the supermarket queue). But when you choose to go to the back and serve, none of that matters anymore. You are free to truly love people. That is Jesus—what a beautiful Servant King.

Jesus is wonderful because he chose the back of the queue and the lowest of places in order to serve anyone who will come to him.

Where do you find it hard to go to the back of the queue and serve? Who could you let push ahead of you today?

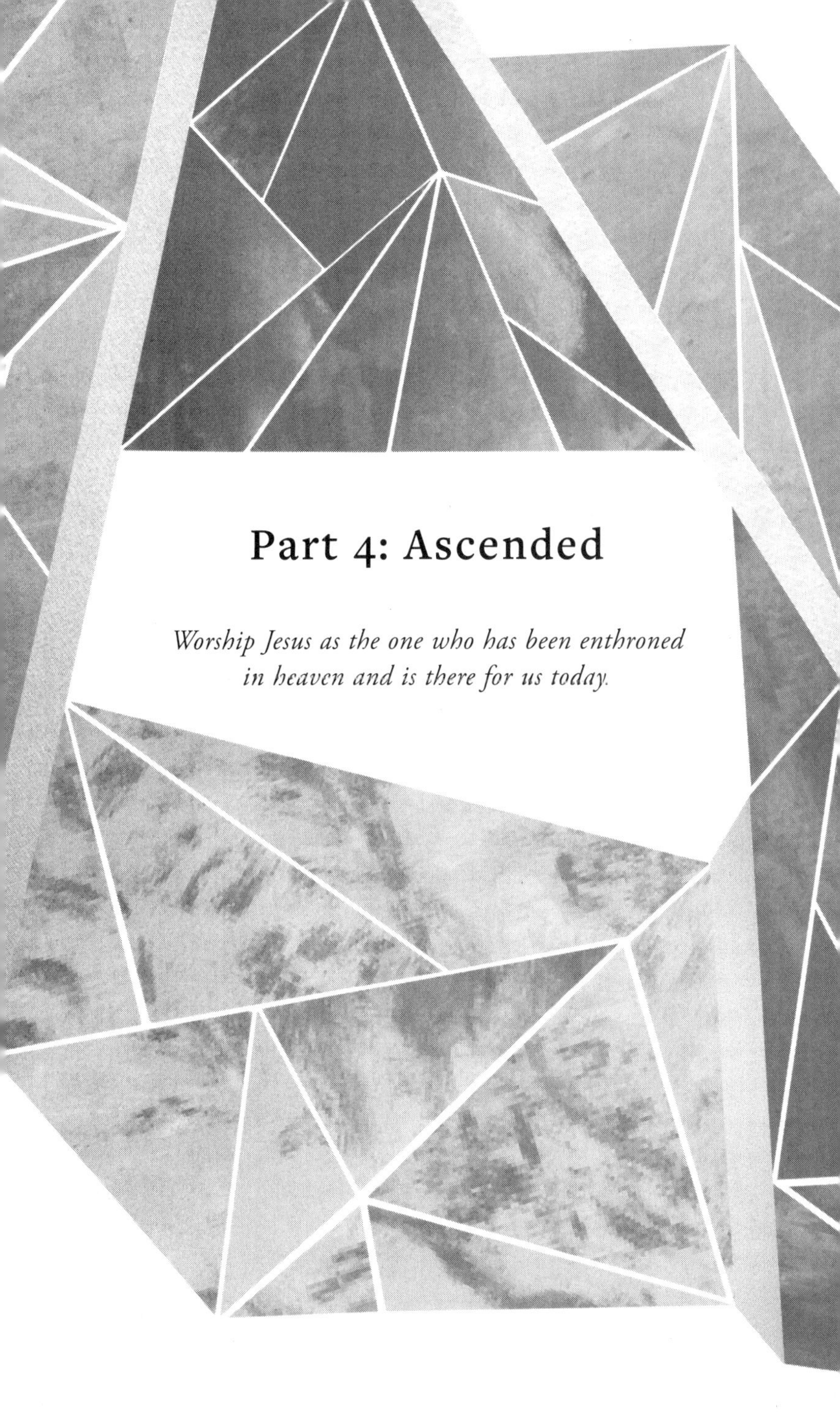

Part 4: Ascended

Worship Jesus as the one who has been enthroned in heaven and is there for us today.

31

Death Defeater

It was impossible for death to keep its hold on him.

Acts 2:24

Death reigned as an undefeated champion over human history. He cast his dark and inevitable shadow over every passing day of every human life.

Death was a champion that had no need to rush; he was more than willing to wait his time. When people became powerful or wealthy, Death did not mind. When people felt like they would live for ever, Death simply smiled. Like a stealthy predator crouching in the grass, he knew that all he had to do was wait. Every tick of the clock whispered the same reality—time will pass and then Death will come. That is just what it means to be human in a world under God's curse. Death reigned.

Of course, Death had his limits; he could not touch the eternal Son of God who dwelt in immortality, but there was plenty of other work to get on with. Then, in an act of breathtaking sacrifice, God became man and entered this cursed world, placing himself in the firing line.

Death could hardly believe what he was seeing—what an opportunity to do some real damage. From the moment Jesus drew his first breath as a baby, Death was stalking him. The clock was ticking. Death was the inescapable end of the line.

There were a few moments in Jesus' life that might have caused Death a brief wobble. On three separate occasions Jesus raised dead people back to life. This was certainly more power than Death was used to dealing with, but surely these were just blips. Jesus might have postponed Death for a few years but each of them would die again. Death remained confident and undefeated.

And then came *the* moment for Jesus. It was earlier than might naturally have been expected; Death came prematurely at the hands of violent men. But Death didn't mind. Whether through violence or sickness or accident or age, Death always had the final word.

As Jesus hung on the cross gasping for air, Death was gleefully poised to gather in one more trophy. As Jesus breathed his final breath, Death stepped in to claim his prize. Like so many who had gone before, Jesus was simply the latest victim of the all-powerful reign of Death.

Tragic. A life ended too soon. So much potential. So much good that he could have achieved. Now he was gone. Consigned to the history books, never to be seen again.

But Death got a terrible shock. There was something different about this man—something Death had never experienced before. When Jesus died, a deeper power was unleashed that was shaking the very fabric of the universe.

There was a rumbling of change that Death was not ready for. The once all-powerful Death was suddenly staring defeat in the face.

In a burst of glorious light, Jesus broke free from the hold of Death and emerged victorious into the stunning reality of a brand new day. That Sunday morning, the sun rose on a new beginning. That Sunday morning, the Son rose to bring about a new era.

Just as light drove back the darkness on the first day of creation, now the Light of the world drove back the darkness of Death to bring the glorious hope of a new world. Behold the conquering, death-defeating High King of heaven.

Ever since that day, the power of Death has been broken. Death still stalks; he still seeks out victims. We still stand at gravesides and weep. We still experience the frustration of bodies that are declining and frail. We still live with the shadow of Death hanging over us and one day each of us will face Death. But because of Jesus, everything has changed.

Death is a defeated enemy. Death has lost his sting. Anyone who is united with Jesus will share in his great victory. Death will not be able to keep hold of us, and we will rise to the life that is far beyond the clutches of sorrow and pain.

Jesus has walked that road already—he has fought that battle and won. Death can bring us pain but he is no longer powerful. Take heart and hold on.

Jesus is wonderful because he has defeated death completely and opened the door to life.

Where do you feel the shadow of death? How does the resurrection of Easter Sunday morning give you hope today?

32

Kingdom Bringing

The kingdom of God has come near.

Mark 1:15

Stories of revolution have always stirred the human heart. Even if you are not a fan of musicals, it is hard not to be moved by the iconic words of the French Revolutionaries in *Les Misérables*, singing with the anger and passion of a people "who will not be slaves again".

An oppressive system. A crushed people. A courageous uprising. A heroic battle. The hope of a new world.

It is a narrative that resonates deep within us. Have you ever wondered why we love these stories? Could it be that these longings point us to something more—that there is a greater revolution that the whole world is aching for? We look around and we see injustice and suffering. We have a sense that things are not the way they should be. We long for change. That is why these words of Jesus are sensationally good news:

The time has come … The kingdom of God has come near. Repent and believe the good news! (Mark 1:15)

Jesus is deliberately using the evocative language of revolution. It might be hard for us to fully appreciate, but this statement is crackling with powerful anticipation. It would have ignited a spark in the hearts of his hearers. A bit of background will help us to see what is happening…

The history of our world is the story of two great revolutions.

The first was the revolution that plunged our world into the grim reality of darkness and death. God had created a beautiful world and he was its good and rightful King. Life in his kingdom meant freedom, light and joy. But humanity was deceived and came to believe the lie that God was a tyrant. They declared independence and established a rival kingdom. They believed that overthrowing God was the key to a more fulfilled and free life. But they were wrong. Here is the problem: you cannot overthrow God because he is God. So now you have two kingdoms: the kingdom of God and the kingdom of this world. The kingdom of light and the kingdom of darkness. The kingdom of life and the kingdom of death.

We live every day with the devastating consequences of that revolution. A great chasm was opened up between heaven and earth. Humanity became enslaved by the selfish pursuit of personal freedom. Each of us is trying to establish our own little kingdom. All the pain and suffering in our world can be traced back to this first revolution. We became enemies of God.

But God was not finished with his world—he had always planned to launch a counter-revolution to win back his creation and set humanity free. It was a relentless refrain that rang out from the prophets. Something is coming. Someone is coming. Revolution is coming. The darkness will be overthrown and injustice will be reversed. Good news will be preached to the poor.

And then, a carpenter from Nazareth, standing by the Sea of Galilee, announced to the world, "The time has come". This is the moment. The kingdom of God has come near. Heaven has invaded earth and the great chasm has been crossed. Light has burst into the darkness and the second revolution has begun.

But this kingdom is not like any that has been seen before. This was not an invasion of hostility to destroy all the enemies; this was an invasion of love that came to rescue the enemies. The kingdom of God is not defined by a tyrannical rule but by a fatherly welcome. It is righteousness in the place of injustice. Love in the place of hate. Forgiveness in the place of revenge. Sacrifice in the place of selfishness. A cross in the place of a palace. Hope in the place of fear.

Here is the kingdom of God on earth. The great revolution of the King who gave his life to save us and now calls us to join him. We no longer need to remain enslaved to the kingdom of darkness. We can turn and embrace the kingdom of light.

We are not just saved for a personal relationship with God. We are not just sitting around waiting for heaven. We are saved to be a part of this kingdom and to live out this revolution of love in our daily lives. We are saved to be a part of this great story and to declare this kingdom to the world.

Jesus is wonderful because he has crossed the chasm and come to earth, bringing his extraordinary kingdom of love.

What will it look like for you to live a revolutionary life today?

33

Enthroned

But about the Son he says, "Your throne,
O God, will last for ever and ever."

Hebrews 1:8

Nebuchadnezzar occupied the most powerful throne in the world. He was the king of Babylon which was the superpower of the day. Yet one night in his bed, he had a dream that troubled him deeply. He saw a statue with a head of gold, a chest of silver, legs of bronze and feet of iron and clay. He knew it was important, but no one could tell him what it meant. He was desperate to know, raging at his wise men and tormented in his thinking.

Meanwhile, Daniel—one of God's people transported to Babylon in Exile—heard about this dream. He prayed and God showed him what it meant. He approached the king and explained the dream. It got off to a great start:

You are that head of gold. (Daniel 2:38)

You can imagine Nebuchadnezzar nodding with approval. But he wasn't ready for the next two words that would strike fear into his heart.

After you… (v 39)

Whenever anyone addressed Nebuchadnezzar they would say, "O King who lives for ever". But these two little words shattered that illusion.

After you will come another kingdom, then another, then another. The throne will keep changing hands. The rulers will come and they will go. After you… After you… After you.

This is the reality of our world. Nations rise and then they fall; they look unshakeable until they are shaken. Where is the Babylonian Empire? Or the Greek Empire? Or the Roman Empire? Or any other historical empire that has faded away? They are crumbled ruins that tourists visit on holiday.

It reminds me of a game we used to play as children. A bar of chocolate was placed in the centre of the circle. Everyone took it in turns to roll a die. If you rolled a six, you ran to the centre, put on a hat, scarf and gloves and then attempted to eat the chocolate with a knife and fork. But it was not possible to enjoy the moment. All the time the clock was ticking, the die was rolling and you knew that your chance would soon be over. Someone else would roll a six and your opportunity would be gone. It still evokes a sense of stress as I recall it.

That is the futility of political power and human thrones; they roll a six and have a brief moment in charge. They roar, grab as much as they can and then they are overthrown and disappear from the stage. It is the story of our world from the very beginning. It continues to be the story of our world today. History is littered with these rulers who had their moment and then were swept away. Power is an illusion that is quickly shattered.

But there was more to the dream—a detail that at first looks so insignificant: a rock. Unimpressive next to the statue, it was easily overlooked. But when this little rock struck the statue, it brought the whole thing crashing down. Then the rock grew to be a huge mountain that filled the whole earth.

Daniel explained to Nebuchadnezzar that this rock was a kingdom that the God of heaven would establish. This is the kingdom that will never be destroyed. This is the throne that will last for ever. What a vision for the future—when the thrones of this world will fall silent and all of humanity will be united under one eternal throne.

But who could ever be entrusted with the throne that ends all thrones? Who could ever occupy a position of such absolute power? In Daniel 7, he sees a glimpse of such a person. Daniel sees a human figure who was led into God's presence and given authority, glory and sovereign power. He is enthroned as King and all the peoples of every language worship him.

Although Daniel never knew his name, he was seeing the glorious ascension of Jesus to his throne.

The ascension of Jesus is a moment of profound historical, political and eternal significance. Jesus wasn't just going home to heaven; he was ascending to the eternal throne of God's kingdom. His throne alone will last for ever.

Sometimes we might feel afraid of the kingdoms of this world. We might fear powerful leaders who seem invincible. But all of them will pass. Their thrones will perish. Someone else will take their place. In a terrifying world, here is what we need to know: as we join our voices to worship Jesus, in whatever language we may speak, we are the fulfilment of the great vision of Daniel 7.

Your throne, O God, will last for ever.

Jesus is wonderful because he has been enthroned as the glorious King for ever and ever.

Why is it foolish to fear (or put our hope in) human leaders who sit on a throne?

34

Glorified

Therefore God exalted him to the highest place.

Philippians 2:9

People walked past Jesus on the dusty streets of Galilee and did not even notice him. They were in the presence of the Son of God and yet they didn't turn their heads. Remarkable. People bumped shoulders with him in the crowded market, they sold him fish, they stood and prayed next to him in the synagogue. All the time they were completely unaware of the glory that lay just below the surface. Even as his popularity and fame grew, people had no idea what they were truly encountering. For a few years of human life, Jesus set aside his eternal glory and walked our road of suffering and pain. His glory was hidden so that he could come close. People were meeting God, and they had no idea!

But there was one brief moment when three of his disciples got a glimpse of something more. Peter, James and

John went up a mountain with Jesus. Suddenly the veil was lifted and Jesus' true glory shone forth. It was breathtaking and unmistakeable. Jesus was transformed from "glory hidden" to "glory revealed". The disciples were blown away—they wanted to pitch their tents and stay on the mountain for ever. But that was not in line with the reason Jesus came. He had a different road to walk.

Jesus was not grasping for status and power. He left those things at the top of the mountain and chose instead to walk the downward path of a servant. This should cause our hearts to worship. He humbled himself, made himself nothing and stepped down from the mountain in order to die in weakness and shame.

For 33 years he lived in this "glory hidden" reality. But at the resurrection, all of that changed. The apostle Paul writes that Jesus was…

> *… appointed the Son of God in power by his resurrection from the dead. (Romans 1:4)*

At the resurrection, the Lord Jesus left behind the glory-hidden existence of frail humanity. He was exalted to the position of "Son of God in power". This is not simply a return to what he was before—it is something brand new. His eternal divine nature has not changed (because God cannot change), but the resurrection marked a turning point in his humanity. Hiddenness gave way to glory. Frailty gave way to power. Death gave way to life.

He has not shed his human body to return to a pre-incarnate state. Rather, his lowly humanity has been transformed into eternal glory. Jesus has now been revealed to the whole world as the magnificent Son of God.

This is why the resurrection matters. Jesus didn't just come back to life; it is not just a happy end to the story. He was taken from the bottom of the mountain and given his rightful place at the top. This is not self-appointed glory. He has been given that honour by the Father.

A shrivelled view of Jesus will lead to a shrivelled confidence, a shrivelled courage and a shrivelled hope for the future. Jesus is no longer on the cross—no longer in the grave. He has been raised to the highest place. He is the Son of God in power.

In our weakness, frailty and death, we desperately need to see the glory of Jesus today. And his glory is for ever.

Jesus is wonderful because he chose humility and has now been glorified.

Where do you find that your view of Jesus is shrivelled and small?

35

Spirit Giver

He will baptise you with the Holy Spirit.

Mark 1:8

Sometimes it feels as if heaven is shut. We ask for help but seem to get no answer. We long for change but feel powerless in the battle. We wish that Jesus was right here walking alongside us, but he is in heaven, and we are on earth. Where can we find help?

Many centuries ago, Isaiah expressed the same longing:

Oh, that you would rend the heavens and come down.
(Isaiah 64:1)

At a time of deep distress, when God seemed distant, Isaiah longed that heaven would be torn open and that God would pour out his Spirit on a dry and barren land. Isaiah wasn't just imagining that heaven was shut. It really was.

Of course, our world wasn't always that way. In the

beginning, the powerful Spirit of God was giving life and bringing joy to all of creation. The first human beings were filled with God's Spirit to be the anointed rulers of God's beautiful world. But they rejected that calling and so the access to heaven was removed. The life-giving Spirit was taken away. The garden that pulsated with life became a wilderness that was polluted by death. So much was lost.

But God was not going to hand over his world completely. The Spirit of God was still working, so he came to specific individuals to empower them for specific tasks. He came to prophets and kings, to musicians and leaders. The life-giving Spirit of heaven was still at work in the wilderness world. There were glimpses, moments, tastes. But it was all so limited. Isaiah and the prophets longed for the day when heaven would be torn open and the Spirit would be unleashed in all his life-giving power. How could that ever be?

That question brings us to the opening chapter of Mark's Gospel. It is no accident that "wilderness" is mentioned four times. Mark wants us to know that Jesus is coming into the world where heaven is closed off and the Spirit is absent. Now, listen to what happens when Jesus comes to be baptised. It is spectacular:

> *Just as Jesus was coming up out of the water, he saw heaven being torn open and the Spirit descending on him like a dove. (Mark 1:10)*

What a moment! Isaiah's longing is now a reality: heaven is torn open and the Spirit is poured out. Jesus is the Spirit-anointed ruler of God's creation. And what will be his work? He will be the one to baptise all of God's people with the Holy Spirit. Everywhere Jesus went, he brought the renewing Spirit of God to a wilderness world. Into death he breathed life. Into the darkness he breathed light.

Mark's Gospel starts with heaven being torn open—and then it ends in exactly the same way. Heaven is torn open again, but this time it is as Jesus dies on the cross. The curtain in the temple is torn from top to bottom. The barrier that barred the way to God is removed.

Here is the gospel: Jesus came to tear heaven open. Jesus died to tear heaven open. Jesus rose to pour out the Spirit of God on all who believe.

On the day of Pentecost, the Spirit was given and the apostle Peter preached:

> *Exalted to the right hand of God, he [Jesus] has received from the Father the promised Holy Spirit and has poured out what you now see and hear. (Acts 2:33)*

The Holy Spirit of God, who filled Jesus and led Jesus and empowered Jesus, has now been given to us. He lives in us and he makes us more like Jesus. He brings life where there is death. He brings renewal where there is decay. He brings transformation and hope where there has been despair.

The battle is intense. The old desires still try to gain control. It is hard and we sometimes feel alone. But the truth is that you are not alone in the fight. Every aspect of following Jesus is done in the Spirit's heavenly power. Everything. We walk in step with him.

Jesus is wonderful because he has torn heaven open and poured out his Spirit.

Where do you feel weakest today? Where do you feel like you are failing? Ask for a deeper reliance on the Spirit of God who lives in you.

36

Firstfruits

*But Christ has indeed been raised from the dead,
the firstfruits of those who have fallen asleep.*

1 Corinthians 15:20

We have an imagination problem. On a freezing cold morning, with the rain lashing down and the wind piercing through our thick coats, it can be hard to imagine the heat of summer where we leave the house in shorts and a T-shirt. Our present experience of reality consumes us. It takes a great deal of effort to imagine anything different.

No wonder we find it hard to imagine the future that God has promised to us through Jesus. Our present experience is all-consuming. A perfect future world might sound like a wonderful idea, but it doesn't feel real. It can quickly become abstract and ethereal. It is supposed to be our great hope but perhaps it slips into a world of make-believe and fairy stories.

The "real" world causes us hurt. The real world throws struggles our way. The real world is still overshadowed by the great enemy of death. Anything beyond this world is relegated to the "less-than-real" category.

The Bible writers clearly have a very different perspective on reality. They are given a Spirit-inspired imagination that enables them to see more. The hope is woven through the narrative, whispered in the poetry and promised in the prophets. Expectant but unseen. Waiting.

Then, early one Sunday morning, all those hopes came into sharp focus. After two days in the grave, Jesus rose from the dead and the future became the present. He was visibly, physically and joyfully alive. He reveals what life looks like on the other side of the grave. He has blazed a trail that one day we will follow.

This is why Jesus is called the firstfruits. I have very little experience of farming, but it seems to me that farmers need great imagination. You need to be able to see beyond the present reality and imagine what the empty field could become. You break up the hard, unyielding ground. It is backbreaking work and often feels futile, but your imagination drives you forward. You scatter the seed, and it is buried underground. It all looks dead. Nothing is happening. But your imagination means that you hold your nerve and keep waiting. On some days it feels bleak. On some days you are gripped by doubt and anxiety. On some days you shed tears but still you wait. And then comes the moment you have been longing for. The very first of your crops bursts forth in fruit and you gather a handful. It is juicy and healthy and abounding with life.

That earliest fruit is so deeply precious because it tells you that more is coming. It fuels your vision of what the future holds and your confidence surges. It shows you that all of your labour has not been in vain. The hoping, working, sweating, and waiting was all worth it because the harvest is coming. You don't yet have everything, but you have the first fruits, and it sends a wave of joy pulsing through your soul. The full harvest is coming.

The first fruits of the harvest show us what to expect. The body of Jesus was raised and that means our bodies will one day be raised. The body of Jesus was made new, so that means our bodies will be made new. He was set free from decay and frustration, so we will be set free from decay and frustration. He was raised in glory, never to die again. And so will we be.

The resurrection of Jesus is real—that means our resurrection hope is real.

As we meditate on the historical fact of Jesus' resurrection, let that fuel your imagination and longing. When your body is creaking and your heart is failing, look forward to the day when your lowly body will be transformed to be like his glorious body (Philippians 3:21).

Can you imagine that? We need to try.

Jesus is wonderful because he is the firstfruits that ignites our imagination for the glorious future God has promised us.

Does your view of the future feel more real or less real than your present life?

37

Advocate

My dear children, I write this to you so that you will not sin. But if anybody does sin, we have an advocate with the Father—Jesus Christ, the Righteous One.

1 John 2:1

We all know that Christians are not supposed to sin anymore. And yet we still do it. It is one of the heartbreaking and painful facts of living as a Christian. The writer of the book of Proverbs describes it as being like a dog returning to its vomit. It is not an image that makes it onto many Christian posters, but it is a reality in many of our hearts.

Ongoing sin unsettles us. It nags away at us and robs us of joy. It holds us back and engulfs us in shame. Jesus has loved us so deeply that he gave his life to rescue us from the kingdom of darkness. He has made us new. He has given us his Spirit. He has done all of this and yet we still find ourselves returning again and again to patterns of behaviour that are ugly and dark. We don't want to. We feel guilty. But we just keep going back.

Sometimes we try to hide our shame—we put on a mask so that no one knows the truth about what is going on. Sometimes we try to fix it—we put new strategies in place and resolve to try harder. Sometimes we excuse it—we act as though it doesn't really matter and it isn't really our fault. Sometimes we give up the fight—but there is a better answer for the times when we sin.

Rather than looking inward and despairing, we need to look upward and see that we have an advocate in heaven. The work of Jesus is not only that he died for us but also that he lives for us.

It is only his presence in heaven that assures us that we are secure. If he took a break, we would be lost. Just think of it—right now, the Lord Jesus is in heaven and he is there on your behalf. It is a terrible thing to stand alone in a court room with no one alongside you and no one to defend you. It is even more terrible if you know you are guilty and you have nowhere to hide.

Hear this: if the Lord Jesus is your Advocate, then you will never stand alone before God. You will never be left to defend yourself and your record of sinful failure. Let me try to bring this home with a bit of imagination: picture yourself sitting in the dock as Jesus rises to his feet to speak on your behalf.

What on earth is he going to say? How can he defend you when your guilt is clear? Will he make excuses for your behaviour? Will he point to the good things you have done with your life? Your heart pounds.

But then, as you wait for him to speak, you notice that he has nail marks in his hands—deep wounds of love that tell the story of a price that has already been paid. A hushed awe descends. The profound meaning of the wounds reverberates around the court. Then Jesus places a nail-pierced hand on your shoulder and declares, "This one is mine".

Nothing more is required. Nothing more is said.

This is what Jesus is doing every moment of every day on our behalf. It is his presence in heaven that guarantees our eternal security. Especially when we sin.

Let me be clear, it would be a terrible distortion to imagine Jesus trying to pacify an angry Father and persuade him to forgive. That is not the case. The only reason we have an Advocate is because the Father provided him. The Son is not persuading the Father to do something he doesn't want to do. The Son is doing precisely what the Father sent him to do.

So, how do we respond to our sin? We do not need to hide it, fix it, excuse it or pay for it. Instead, we trust the one who bears the wounds of love and eternally lives to plead for us.

Jesus is wonderful because he is always in heaven on our behalf so that we can have hope and security.

When you sin, where do you place your confidence to put things right?

38

Intercessor

Jesus … is at the right hand of God
and is also interceding for us.

Romans 8:34

Self-confidence is a dangerous poison for Christians to drink. The key to our survival is not found in our ability to handle whatever is thrown at us. Rather, it comes from the profound truth that Jesus is praying for us.

We are weak but Jesus is praying for us. We are vulnerable but Jesus is praying for us. We are in danger, but Jesus is praying for us.

This is not a vague and abstract idea—we can see a concrete example of it when Jesus prays for his friend Simon Peter. It was the night before Good Friday and Peter is facing the fiercest trial of his life. The danger is real but Simon Peter just doesn't see it. He is absolutely confident in his own ability to handle the pressure: "I will never disown you" (Mark 14:31). And in that moment, I think he really meant it.

But Jesus sees things very differently. He turns to Simon Peter and says:

> *Simon, Simon, Satan has asked to sift all of you as wheat. But I have prayed for you, Simon, that your faith may not fail. And when you have turned back, strengthen your brothers. (Luke 22:31-32)*

The trial that is coming is far beyond Simon Peter's ability. He does not have the strength to handle this. There is an enemy who is resolutely set upon destroying him. Satan wants to sift him—it is a graphic picture of the enemy's hostile intentions. When you sift wheat, you shake it so that the rubbish is swept away and only the good remains. Satan is plotting to shake Simon Peter so violently that he will be broken to pieces, exposed and swept away from Jesus.

Make no mistake, this enemy is powerful, but he is not all-powerful. Notice that he has to ask permission before he can do anything to God's children. The evil intentions of Satan must bow before the sovereign rule of the true King. What Satan intends for harm will be repurposed by the Lord Jesus for the ultimate good of his precious disciple. It is crucial for us to see that Jesus does not take Simon Peter out of the trial but instead prays for him in the time of shaking.

Simon Peter will stumble. When the day of shaking comes, he will find himself intensely tested beyond his ability to stand. Satan is a crafty enemy who knows where to attack. Courage is not Peter's downfall—it is shame. He is ready to fight but not to embrace weakness. It is not a Roman soldier but a little servant girl who proves too much for him. The enemy has set his trap; Simon will deny Jesus. And as the cock crows, Simon's world collapses into despairing sobs of failure. He is on the brink of being swept away—but Jesus has prayed for him.

Simon Peter's self-confidence was shattered that night. But he saw more clearly than ever his desperate need of Jesus.

Just as Jesus prayed for Simon Peter, so he prays for all his people. We might prefer it if Jesus simply protected us from any times of shaking. We might prefer Jesus to muzzle the enemy so we can cruise through life with no struggles. But Jesus has greater ambitions for us—he does not take us out of the trials, but he prays for us in our trials.

Later on in the New Testament, it talks about Jesus this way:

Jesus … is at the right hand of God and is also interceding for us. (Romans 8:34)

It is when we are severely shaken that our faith is revealed to be genuine. It is when we come to the end of our own ability that we are forced to abandon trust in ourselves and rest more deeply on Jesus.

Hear Jesus speak to you those precious words he said to Simon Peter that night: *I have prayed for you that your faith may not fail.*

Jesus is wonderful not because he removes our trials, but because he prays for us in every trial.

Where do you feel the shaking and testing of your faith? How does it help to know that Jesus is praying for you?

39

Head

God placed all things under his feet and appointed him to be head over everything for the church.

Ephesians 1:22

It is an undeniable fact of nature that it is a good thing for a body to have a head. Without one we would be far less effective at… living. We use the image of a headless chicken to convey the complete chaos of being out of control. Our bodies need a head in order to save us from disorder and death. Our world is just the same. It is fragmented and chaotic, full of billions of people pulling in different directions and creating conflict of tragic proportions.

Dreamers dream and poets imagine and politicians promise and all of us long for a world of perfect harmony. But how could that ever be possible?

Think about the excitement of a new box of Lego. It has a shiny picture of a castle on the front. It has so much potential. But when you open it, you are confronted with chaos—a random mess of brightly coloured pieces. It makes no sense at all. You can almost hear the bricks groaning, "We were made for much more than this. Help us!" In order for the pieces to fulfil their true destiny, they need to be brought together by a builder. Lego without a builder is a painful mess (think bare feet on the scattered pieces). But in the hands of a skilful child (or adult!) it becomes something beautiful.

Our world is groaning for someone to come and put it back together again. Many of us have stepped on the painful shards of reality and now carry the scars. Our world needs someone who can bring beauty out of the brokenness, meaning out of the mess, unity out of the chaos. Our world needs a Head.

According to Ephesians 1, this is precisely what God is doing in the world. He isn't only saving individuals for a personal relationship with Jesus—God has even greater ambitions for this broken world. Listen to how it is explained:

> *[God is working to] bring unity to all things in heaven and on earth under Christ. (v 10)*

> *God placed all things under his feet and appointed him to be head over everything for the church. (v 22)*

It is crystal clear that the hope for our world is Jesus Christ as the one Head under which all things will find their rightful and joyful place. This is the great purpose for which God created all things. All fractures healed, all pain ended, all divisions destroyed.

No mere human leader could ever be trusted with that position. It would be dangerous and impossible. But

Jesus Christ is the perfectly wise, beautifully gentle and completely good Head. Our world will be released from the groaning when all things find their rightful place under his great headship. All the divisions will be healed, all the fractures will be repaired, all the hostility will be ended and the whole universe united—only Christ can do that.

And here is the surprise: this is not just a future reality that we have to sit and wait for. God has begun that uniting work already in the church. The church is Christ's body, and he is the Head. It is in the church that all sorts of people, from all sorts of backgrounds, with all sorts of ambitions are woven together into one great whole.

Church is an awesome thing when it is functioning with one Head. It is a tragedy when churches lose connection with the Head. Churches can become chaotic and messy or, even worse, they can become torn apart by power plays and rivalries. Like the terrible multi-headed beasts of mythology, churches can become horrible distortions of the body God intended. None of us are the head that our local church needs.

There is one Head in the church and our unity depends entirely on remaining connected with him. When Jesus' wisdom, love, patience, forgiveness and grace are flowing through our veins, we will put on display to the world a little glimpse of what God has planned for this universe. We will smash down walls, cross boundaries, crucify personal tastes and comfort, and we will experience the joy of unity.

This is so precious to Jesus that he prayed this for his church on the night before his death. He prayed "that all of them may be one, Father, just as you are in me and I am in you" (John 17:21).

Jesus is wonderful because he is the Head who will unite the whole world.

Where do you feel disunity most keenly at the moment? Ask Jesus to bring all things together under his loving headship.

40

Wise

Christ the power of God and the wisdom of God.

1 Corinthians 1:24

When Jesus was just a boy, we read that he "was filled with wisdom". Nice. It might be easy to smile and move on.

But we need to stop for a moment—that statement is loaded with theological weight. Wisdom is a major stream of thought that runs right through the story of the Bible and this child is being located within it. When we trace it back to its source, we will find that wisdom has a very long history.

There is a beautiful and mysterious poem in Proverbs 8 where wisdom introduces herself to the world. She tells us that her eternal source is God. He is the Father who gave her birth. Wisdom is not just an abstract principle but can be thought of as a person who flows from the very being of God. She also tells us that she was at God's side in creation; it was by wisdom that this world was designed. The world wasn't formed by random and chaotic chance but by powerful and creative wisdom. And she was rejoicing as the world came into being. Wisdom was full of vigour and life as she delighted in what she saw. She sounds amazing.

She also sounds strangely familiar. In a poetic and powerful way, she seems to bear a striking similarity to the eternal Son of God. Wisdom is personified in this beautiful woman and then is perfectly revealed in the person of Jesus. He is the perfect wisdom of God.

This eternal wisdom was gifted to humanity to enable us to lovingly rule the world that God had made. But, in a crazy distortion of reality, humanity pursued an alternative wisdom and, as a result, fell into the clutches of darkness and folly. It is important to see that our first parents ate the fruit in the garden because it was "desirable for gaining wisdom" (Genesis 3:6). Can you see the twisted tragedy of human sin? We grasped for something we already had. Rather than humbly embracing the wisdom of God, we proudly grabbed at something "more". This is the desperate plight of humanity. We have set ourselves up against the God who always opposes the proud.

There were some moments of light in the Bible's wisdom story, most notably in the time of King Solomon. He rejected the proud human wisdom that seeks glory and wealth and instead humbly asked for God's wisdom so that he might rule carefully. He looks like a human who is being what humans are meant to be. But even Solomon could not turn the tide of human folly and ended up succumbing to pride and false worship.

Wisdom was never about a simple set of rights and wrongs. Wisdom is an eternal principle woven through creation. Wisdom is knowing that this is God's world. Wisdom is the humble discernment to make the best choices in complex and difficult situations. Wisdom is knowing that humility will always be better than pride and that sacrifice will always be more powerful than greed.

At the appointed time, a child comes along who is "filled with wisdom". He is the one who is greater than Solomon (Luke 11:31). He is the one who is fully equipped with what he needs to navigate God's world in the way we were always supposed to.

Jesus confronted the arrogant human pride that he saw all around him. He confounded the wisdom of this world. People could not understand him; he did not fit into their categories. He never tried to impress people or to speak to gain applause from the crowd. Yet his teaching was different to anything anyone had ever heard. Every time he opened his mouth, the wisdom of God poured out.

Human wisdom grasps for power and glory. Jesus, the eternal wisdom of God, let it all go. He gave himself up to suffer on a cross to save his people. The world looks and mocks; the world sees weakness and folly. But for those who look with the eyes of humility, there is something far bigger going on.

Here is the very wisdom of God, the one eternally born of the Father, offering a way for humanity to escape the slavery of pride and embrace the wisdom of God.

We spend so much of our lives trying to be wise in our own eyes—financially wise, academically wise, practically wise. But all true wisdom starts here. Come and gaze again upon the man hanging lifeless on the cross. Do you see weakness? Or do you see wisdom? Will you humble yourself in worship and embrace the eternal wisdom of God?

Jesus is wonderful because he is the beautiful wisdom of God.

In what ways do you seek to be wise in your own eyes? How can you embrace the wisdom of Jesus?

Part Five: Returning

Worship Jesus as the one who will return to put all things right.

The Man

This same Jesus…

Acts 1:11

The brothers hadn't seen Joseph for many, many years. Their last glimpse was of him being dragged away as a slave. They had left him for dead. Life had carried on. Joseph was consigned to history. But years later, they received the shock of their lives. In a state of starvation, they travelled to Egypt to beg for food, where they found themselves confronted by a powerful Egyptian ruler who held their lives in his hands. They were at his mercy. He was magnificent and glorious and they fell down before him. Then they heard these words, "I am Joseph!" (Genesis 45:3).

It was the same man that they had grown up with, the same man they had known so well. The brother they had despised and rejected now stood before them in majestic glory. The lowly Joseph seemed so utterly different to the glorified Joseph. The brothers would never have dreamed it could ever be the same person, until Joseph opened his mouth and told them.

This story sets the pattern for a far greater reality. One day Jesus will return, and he will be magnificent and glorious. He will come with eyes of blazing fire and robes of golden majesty. His voice will be like the sound of mighty waters and his face will shine more brightly than the sun. He will hold our very lives in his hand, and we will fall down before him.

But here is the key for us today: it will be the same man who walked this earth.

This was emphasised for the disciples on the day Jesus returned to heaven. Two angels appeared and told them:

> *This same Jesus, who has been taken from you into heaven, will come back in the same way you have seen him go into heaven. (Acts 1:11)*

During his time on earth, the Lord Jesus entered into the lowly weakness of our frail, decaying bodies. But he will return with a body that is glorified and eternal. On the cross, Jesus shuddered and gasped for breath. His body was battered and bruised. He died. But when he returns, he will have a body that is breathtaking in its power and beauty.

He was a lowly man; now he is the glorified man, but he is still *the man.* He has not stopped being human. The glorified body we will one day see is the same body that once suffered in our place. And not only will he come with the same (but now glorified) body, he will also come with the same character. Jesus is still the man who is gentle and kind. He is still the man who stops for the blind beggar and notices the widow.

Sometimes we might be tempted to somehow imagine that the Jesus of the Gospels is relatable and kind, but that the Jesus who will return will be vengeful and terrifying. But that cannot be, because Jesus is the same yesterday, today and for ever (Hebrews 13:8). When Jesus comes to put an end to wickedness and to restore all of creation, he will do it with precisely the same heart that we see on every page of the Gospels. He will defeat his enemies through the power of sacrificial love. He will drive out darkness by unleashing his glorious light. He will bind up the weak, the oppressed and the poor. The perfect man who we meet in the Gospels is the same man who will come again. This is why we can trust him.

Jesus is not coming to rescue us from being human. He is the perfect man who is redeeming us to become fully human. Not only will Jesus be the same Jesus—you will be the same you. Our weak and frail bodies will be transformed to be like his glorious body. We will see him and love him and worship him with perfected bodies. What a great day that will be.

Jesus is wonderful because he is still the man Christ Jesus and will come back to finish what he has started.

Spend some time meditating on the future return of Jesus. You could read chapter 1 of Revelation. How does it help you to know that this is the same Jesus?

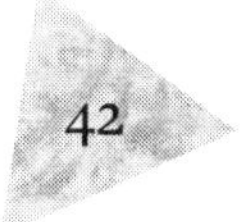

The Master

His master replied, "Well done, good and faithful servant! You have been faithful with a few things; I will put you in charge of many things. Come and share your master's happiness!"

Matthew 25:21

Let's be honest, the word "master" is a hard word to hear. It can conjure up terrible images of cruelty and injustice. The brutal slave trader treating people as property to be used for his own advantage. Or the relentless boss who drives their employees into the ground in the pursuit of more profit. Or the manipulative friend who wants to control everyone around them for their own personal gain. This is called exploitation—and it is always wrong. It should make us shudder when we see this instinct in our world. And it should make us shudder when we see it in our own hearts.

But there is another sort of Master who is driven by love. Before Jesus calls us to serve him, he willingly chose to serve us. (See chapter 30 on Jesus as Servant.) We used to be slaves to darkness; sin was a master that ruthlessly exploited us and caused us great harm. But Jesus came to set us free. We must understand that to be a servant of Jesus is to be truly loved and truly free. Jesus is only our Master because he first gave everything to serve us.

He is our Master and we are his servants, but he will never exploit us. Rather, he entrusts us with the extraordinary privilege of being part of his great work in the world. In Matthew 25:14-30 Jesus tells a wonderful story to help us see the privilege.

Firstly, the master entrusts his great wealth to his servants. He brings them into his work and shares it with them. And even here he is loving and kind; he gives each one only what they are able to manage. One servant gets five bags of gold, one gets two bags, and the last gets one bag. This is not favouritism, it is the kind action of a loving master. He does not dump a burden on people and then abandon them to drown under the impossible weight of the task. He knows his servants and only gives us as much responsibility as we can carry.

When the master has left, Mr Five-Bags enthusiastically gets to work. He is not miserable but joyful to be entrusted with such a great privilege. He works and earns five more bags. It all flows out of his love for his master.

Then comes my favourite character in any of Jesus' stories: Mr Two-Bags. It would have been so easy for him to feel annoyed because he was given less. We can so readily spend our time looking at all the things we don't have—the gifts, the money, the opportunities. But Mr Two-Bags looks at what he does have and gets on with serving. With the same joy, the same privilege and the same enthusiasm.

What has Jesus entrusted you with in order that you can serve him? Don't stress about what you don't have and embrace being a two-bag Christian! It is a glorious thing to be an ordinary servant of Jesus entrusted with work to do.

But Mr One-Bag sees things differently. He does not love his master and feels exploited. He has his own plans and so he buries the gold and gets on with life.

Then comes the return of the master. Imagine the joy of Mr Five-Bags. He rushes to show what he has done and experiences the wonderful praise from the master, "Well done" (v 21). Can you imagine hearing anything better than that? All the hard work, the cost, the struggle—it all becomes worth it in the smile of Jesus. And the result is that the master shares all that he has with the servant. This is how you know it is not exploitation. Jesus is the Master who will share all of his riches with you.

Then comes (my hero) Mr Two-Bags. He is treated exactly the same. He does not receive less; he has lovingly worked hard, and he shares the same joy.

But the return of the master is a terrible day for Mr One-Bag. He digs up the gold, and with grubby hands he angrily hands it back. There is no joy and no love. He accuses the master of being an exploiter. It is shameful.

The master responds with sobering words. The servant will lose what he has. He will be excluded from the kingdom. He will be shut out of the joy. Please see this carefully: the problem is not his failure to work. The problem is his failure to love.

Jesus does not want our money; he wants our hearts.

Do you love Jesus? Will you joyfully take whatever he has entrusted to you and put it to work for his glory? Nothing brings more joy to the heart of the Master.

Jesus is wonderful because he is the kind Master who entrusts his work to us so that we can joyfully share in his riches.

What has God given you that you could invest in his great kingdom?

43

The Warrior

The Lord *is a warrior; the* Lord *is his name.*

Exodus 15:3

Jesus doesn't always fit into the neat boxes we create for him. In Revelation 19 he is described as the Warrior who will come riding on a white horse and wage war against his enemies.

That is a little uncomfortable for most of us. It feels a very long way from the Jesus we meet in the Gospels. Whatever happened to the gentle Lamb who laid down his life in perfect humility? Look closely at the rider and you will recognise all the beauty we have already seen in the Lamb. There is a complete and glorious continuity between the Jesus of history and the Warrior of Revelation 19. We need to get this clear or we will end up with two versions of Jesus that leave us confused and unsettled.

There is a theme of war that runs through the Bible. Many people find the violence of the Old Testament to be very troubling. We instinctively prefer the "nice" Jesus who told us to love our enemies. We breathe a sigh of relief and are grateful that we live this side of the cross. Our moral compass is set. War is wrong and Jesus is all about love and peace. Phew.

Except that this just isn't what you find in the Bible. Not all wars are the same. If we can learn to distinguish this carefully, we will be taken deeper into the beauty of Jesus the Lamb who is also the Warrior.

There is a type of war that is all about fighting to crush the weak and elevate the strong. It is about gaining superiority. Human history is littered with these sorts of brutal conquests. These are the wars that have torn our world to shreds and where the weakest suffer the most.

But there is another reason to go to war. Notice that Jesus is called "Faithful and True" (v 11). When he comes to wage war, the key issue is justice not conquest. In other words, he is not crushing the weak to elevate the strong—he is bringing down the strong to liberate the weak. That is how the kingdom of God works.

God has no need to establish his military superiority—as if humanity could ever threaten him. God is not trying to keep hold of his throne and crown—that is untouchable. But God will absolutely come to the aid of the weak in order to bring justice to the oppressed.

The kingdom of God is good news for the poor but it spells disaster for the arrogant, the wicked and the strong. God sees with blazing clarity what is true and right. His eyes see the very motives of our hearts. Whenever God wages war in the Bible it is a question of justice for the weak and freedom for the slave.

Notice in verse 13 that he arrives at the battle with a robe already dipped in blood. He will make war against the enemy but only as the Lamb who is already stained with the blood of his own sacrificial love. He will trample the enemy in the winepress of God's wrath but only as the Lamb who was first trampled there for us. This is unlike any warrior the world has ever seen.

He does not wield the sword of human violence in his hand, but rather the sword of truth comes from his mouth (v 15). It is the glorious gospel of love and justice that will ultimately bring down the enemy. Jesus comes proclaiming his eternal kingdom of truth and grace and all the little kingdoms of this world will come crashing down.

There will not be a great battle. There will not be a long and tortuous war. The Warrior-Lamb will appear, he will declare his great kingdom and the enemy will be finished. Don't get me wrong, it will be a terrible day for the arrogant and the proud. They will be struck down and punished. But don't blame the Warrior—just look at his robe, listen to his word. He is the Lamb who triumphs by his blood.

In a world of injustice and violence, it is spectacularly good news that there is a Warrior who will come with magnificent justice and will overcome all his enemies by his sacrificial love. People will not be able to stand before the sheer power of his kingdom of grace.

Jesus is wonderful because he is the Warrior who fights with justice and truth.

How does it comfort you today to know that Jesus is the Warrior?

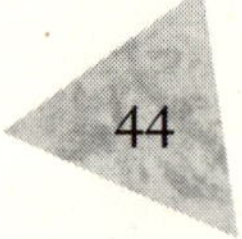

44

The Harvester

So he who was seated on the cloud swung his sickle over the earth, and the earth was harvested.

Revelation 14:16

When it comes to farming, timing is critical. There is a precise moment when the harvest must be gathered in. If you pick too early, the crop is not ready and good plants are wasted. But if you pick too late, the whole thing starts to spoil.

Harvest is the focal point of the farmer's year. It is the culmination of months of preparation and back-breaking work. You wait. And wait. You hold your nerve for the perfect moment, and then you joyfully gather in the abundance.

This is the picture that is repeatedly used in the Bible to describe the future of our world. The present age in which we live is building up to a glorious harvest day. But the imagery of harvest in the Bible is double sided. On the one side is a joyful encouragement to the scattered people of God—they will be gathered together from the four corners of the world and will be united in worship before the throne. The flipside of this harvest is that it stands as a warning to the proud and rebellious. There is a day of judgment, when the harvest is ripe, and the enemies of God will be cut down and removed for ever.

Harvest is a gathering of the good crop and a removal of the bad. It is a decisive and final moment of separation.

When John the Baptist introduced the world to Jesus the Messiah, he described him as the great harvester:

> *His winnowing fork is in his hand to clear his threshing-floor and to gather the wheat into his barn, but he will burn up the chaff with unquenchable fire. (Luke 3:17)*

John the Baptist was very clear about the double-sided harvest that Jesus would reap. But as John watched the ministry of Jesus unfold, it left him puzzled. There was plenty of gathering but not much burning. It even left him wondering whether Jesus really was the Messiah. (See Matthew 11:3.)

Instead of dishing out punishments in his time on earth, Jesus showed love for the wicked. All who were willing to hear were brought into the great barn of God's kingdom. This is the glorious grace of the days in which we live. The final day has not yet come. Now is the day of salvation. Now is the year of the Lord's favour.

Still the Harvester waits for the final decisive day of separation. Then Revelation 14 takes up the motif in powerful and vivid imagery. We see a figure sitting on a cloud (a symbol of the divine), he is called the Son of Man (sounds familiar) and he is wearing a crown of gold. Once again, we are confronted by Jesus, the heroic Lamb of God who stands at the centre of all human history.

He has waited and waited, but now we are told that "the time to reap has come, for the harvest of the earth is ripe" (v 15). The day will not come a moment too early, nor a day too late. At just the right time, the Lord Jesus will swing the sickle, and all his people will be gathered to him. It will be a wonderful day of joy.

Then there is a second harvest in Revelation 14. This time an angel of judgment swings the sickle, and the grapes are gathered and thrown into the winepress of God's wrath. The winepress is trampled and blood flows out. This is not a comfortable image. It is tempting to try and avoid it. But it comes from the Old Testament prophets and describes God's punishment of his enemies. This is not vindictive and malicious, rather, this is God's justice on the wicked.

God has already provided the way of escape. Jesus has already been trampled in order that we might find freedom. But for those who have refused to come, they will be handed over to judgment.

Sometimes it seems that the proud grow strong and tall. Sometimes those who oppress others seem to thrive and flourish. Sometimes those who ignore God seem to be far more successful than those who live by faith. Sometimes we wonder why we even bother living for the kingdom of God.

The book of Revelation calls us to look ahead and live in the light of the future day that is coming. It is only then that the true harvest will be revealed. For those who have lived by faith as citizens of the kingdom of God, it will be the day when we are gathered up and will enter into the fullness of eternal joy.

Jesus is wonderful because he is the patient Harvester who is waiting for the day when he will gather in his glorious harvest.

How can we make the most of the days of grace in which we live as we wait for the final harvest?

45

The Bridegroom

The wedding of the Lamb has come
and his bride has made herself ready.

Revelation 19:7

The world began with a wedding in a garden. And the world will end with a wedding in a garden. There is a wonderful symmetry in the Bible story. Two gardens. Two weddings. Much joy. Adam and Eve. Then Christ and his church.

The connection between these two weddings is described as a "profound mystery" (Ephesians 5:32). That doesn't mean it is a secret that is impossible to work out—rather it means it is a deeply precious truth that can only be properly unravelled in the coming of Jesus. It means that human marriage was always intended to point towards (and then be swallowed up by!) a far greater marriage.

Let's unpick the connection between these two weddings in a bit more detail.

The first bridegroom was the man, Adam. He had been formed from the dust of the earth to care for and to protect the Garden of Eden. But he was not enough to fulfil the purpose of humanity alone. He needed someone to be his friend, his partner, his equal, his opposite. So God acted to create the first woman. Adam was placed into a deep sleep and a hole was pierced in his side. The man was wounded; a red river of blood flowed from the hole. A rib was removed, and the hole was closed up. God took that blood-stained rib and from that sacrifice he created a beautiful bride for the man.

There is a whole heap of truth about human marriage contained in that account, but we miss the point if we fail to see the profound mystery of the ultimate marriage.

The second Bridegroom is the man Jesus Christ. He was formed in the womb of a virgin. He lived a life of perfect love, but in his humanity he never entered into a marriage covenant. That was because God intended to create for him a far greater bride. At the cross, Jesus descended into the deep sleep of death. A hole was pierced in his side. He was wounded and the bright red blood flowed out for all to see. And it was there, in that costly act of sacrifice, that God created a beautiful bride called the church.

The marriage of a man and a woman has far deeper significance than we ever imagined. It is not just a cultural institution that humanity invented for the greater good of society. It cannot simply be redefined or written off as outdated and old-fashioned. Every human marriage (whether people know it or not) proclaims the far greater love story of Christ and his church. Every human wedding is pointing forward to the end of the world.

This love story has a long history. In Exodus 6:7 God promised his people:

> *I will take you as my own people, and I will be your God.*

This was a marriage covenant. God describes himself as the Bridegroom who delights over his bride (Isaiah 62:5). It is a picture of extraordinary intimacy between God and his people.

The tragic reality is that time and again the people spurn God's love and chase after other lovers. It is wicked and it is painful. The people were filthy and unfit for God—he would be completely within his rights to divorce his people and send them away for ever. The marriage is hanging by a thread.

But God is not willing to let the marriage die. When Jesus calls himself the Bridegroom (in Mark 2:19) he is claiming to be God coming for his bride. By his sacrificial death on the cross, he creates a purified, radiant and perfect bride. He did not come searching for an attractive bride that he could love. He came to an unattractive people and died to transform them into his stunning bride.

Jesus does not love his bride because she is lovely. Rather, his love has made his bride lovely. His death washes us clean. His sacrifice makes us worthy. His love will extend to any who will come to him. Jesus is forming the church to be his eternal bride.

The day that he returns will be the wedding day. He will appear in glory. There will be joy and singing:

Hallelujah!
For our Lord God Almighty reigns.
Let us rejoice and be glad
and give him glory!
For the wedding of the Lamb has come,
and his bride has made herself ready. (Revelation 19:6-7)

There is a wedding day coming. If you belong to Jesus, then you will not be a spectator but a joyful participant. It is a day to anticipate, a day to dream about, a day to get ready for.

Jesus is wonderful because he is the Bridegroom who died to create the church and one day he will return to marry her.

How does the promise of this future wedding day help you to live faithfully for Jesus today?

The Dragon Slayer

The great dragon was hurled down.

Revelation 12:9

In recent times, there has been an effort to rehabilitate the public image of dragons. Rather than fire-breathing monsters that pose a terrifying threat to humanity, they have become misunderstood creatures that just need to be trained and embraced.

That idea might make for a good children's film, but the Bible's take is more blunt. The dragon imagery is used to depict the devastating enemy that stands opposed to God and all of his plans. He appears as the serpent in Genesis 3 and as the dragon in Revelation 12. He is called Satan, the devil—an angelic being, who was gripped with pride and rebelled against God and then set out to destroy everything God had made.

The dragon has two great aims. Firstly, he is a deceiver. Jesus refers to him as "a liar and the father of lies"

(John 8:44). Secondly, he is a destroyer; Jesus says he has been a murderer from the beginning. These are his operational tactics: to deceive and to destroy. He has no other weapons in his arsenal.

So, the dragon flatters and flirts with humanity. He is a con artist who offers people a version of reality that is not true. He sets himself up against the God of truth and twists God's word in order to lead people into unbelief and pride. All lies can be traced back to him as the source. False propaganda is particularly effective with people who are all too willing to have their egos flattered and their appetites satisfied. He has been working to cast this spell on humanity since the Garden of Eden. His deception has been disastrously effective.

And when the lies don't work, he will simply lash out to cause as much harm as possible. He hates all of God's image-bearers and especially those who would love God. You can see his hand in the very first murder when Cain killed his brother, Abel. And he has been continuing to stir up violence ever since.

This is the dragon. He has been deceiving and destroying and has caused untold harm. But in the face of this enemy the gospel holds out great hope. In 1 John 3:8 it says, "The reason the Son of God appeared was to destroy the devil's work."

Jesus came to defeat the dragon, but he doesn't overcome the dragon by becoming a more violent dragon with superior strength. Instead, he defeats the dragon by being the Lamb. It is so counterintuitive to a world that is obsessed with power. In a battle between a dragon and a lamb there is only one winner—the lamb will be ripped to pieces and his blood will be poured out. But here is the great paradox: it is the very blood that the dragon draws from the lamb that is the means of the dragon's great defeat (Revelation 12:11) The moment when the dragon seemed to be winning was the precise moment when his defeat was sealed.

Jesus destroyed Satan by deploying his great weapons of truth and love. At the cross, Satan was dealt a fatal blow. He is mortally wounded but he has not yet been fully destroyed. He still prowls the earth like a roaring lion looking for those that he can ruin. He still seeks to deceive the nations with his flattery and lies.

But his final defeat is inevitable. When Jesus returns, he will complete the work he began at the cross. Jesus is the truth, and that will always be more powerful than lies. Jesus is pure love and that will always be more powerful than murder. So Jesus will win and the great dragon will be cast down to the place of eternal punishment that he fully deserves.

We are still in danger of falling for his flattery and lies. We may still hear his violent roar and find our hearts shaking. But we do not need to fear—Jesus is the Dragon Slayer. We are kept safe as we fill ourselves with the truth of Jesus. We are protected as we rest in his gentle love.

Jesus is wonderful because he is the humble Lamb who has defeated the treacherous dragon.

Where do you find your heart is deceived by the dragon's lies? How does his defeat bring you hope and strength?

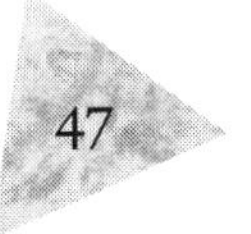

The Peace Bringer

They will beat their swords into ploughshares and
their spears into pruning hooks.
Nation will not take up sword against nation,
nor will they train for war any more.

Isaiah 2:4

World peace has always stood as the ultimate benchmark in human progress. We award the Nobel Prize to those who contribute in some way to this utopian dream of the future. We develop alliances, we negotiate treaties, we build bigger armies—all in the name of protecting this fragile thing we call peace. But just below the surface, the threat of war simmers. Everyone ultimately wants peace, but it seems to be an impossible dream.

We find the same dynamic in our personal relationships. Our words become weapons that unleash conflict, rivalry, strife and discord. We ache for peace, but it seems very distant.

The Bible has an important take on this. Peace is elusive because we have abandoned the one thing that could unite us. Humanity was created to be united in worship and love for God. That vertical love was to overflow in our relationships with one another. But as soon as we removed God and placed ourselves at the centre, we made peace impossible. I may want peace, but I only want it on my terms.

Undoubtedly, there have been towering figures throughout history who have dared to dream that peace was within our grasp. There are beautiful stories that shine brightly against the war-torn wreckage of the human landscape. But despite the glimmers, the legacy of thousands of years of human impact on our planet has been a litany of war, horror and pain.

Even when there have been times of relative peace, it is tense and is mainly achieved through the threat of greater military power. If the only reason I don't fight my neighbour is because I am scared that they might annihilate me, that doesn't really count as peace. But how could we hope for anything more?

Isaiah preached a radical vision of humanity completely united 700 years before the birth of Jesus. In a time of huge political conflict and military superpowers battling for control, he preached about a different type of peace. Isaiah spoke of a world that is so united that no one needs weapons anymore; the swords are instead beaten into tools for farming (2:4). Peace that doesn't need weapons is the sort of peace that God intends for this world.

For Isaiah, this spectacular vision revolved around a promised, Spirit-filled King who would be born as the

Prince of Peace. To cut a long story short, this is Jesus. But in what sense has Jesus done anything to move us closer to the great vision of Isaiah? More than you might think—the plan has already begun.

For a start, at no point in his earthly ministry did he ever pick up a weapon to harm another human being. Not a sword, not a stone, not even a clenched fist. He establishes the great kingdom of God without a shot being fired. Even as they wield weapons against him, he remains defenceless and weak. Yet this is the new power of God that fights a new kind of war to bring a new kind of peace. As Jesus rises from the dead, he demonstrates that the kingdom of God will ultimately outlast the violent kingdoms of this world.

He called his followers to do the same: to love their enemies, to forgive wrong rather than fight for revenge. This is the kingdom of God that Jesus came to bring. This powerful new dynamic is already at play among those who belong to this Prince of Peace.

When Peter lashed out with a sword in the Garden of Gethsemane, Jesus rebuked him. That is not the way his kingdom comes. The early church was an unarmed revolutionary movement. Their power was not military or political or financial; it was the irrepressible power of love.

We still live in a world of human sin. Sadly, human weapons are still needed to restrain evil and protect the weak. But the kingdom of God is only built up when we lay down our weapons and embrace the way of love. The kingdom will continue to advance as the church walks in the way of Jesus. Until the final day, when Jesus will return to fully establish this radical revolution of peace. Will you join in?

Jesus is wonderful because he is establishing an eternal kingdom of peace that has no need for weapons.

Where do you need to learn to lay down your "weapons" in your own relationships?

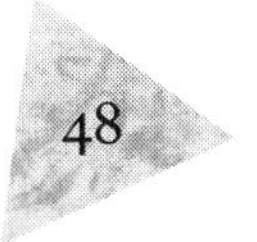

The Tear Wiper

He will wipe every tear from their eyes.

Revelation 21:4

Sometimes we try to hide them. Sometimes we just can't stop them. Sometimes they roll silently down our cheeks. Other times they come with uncontrollable sobbing. Sometimes they take us by surprise. But at other times they seem to be a daily experience. However they might come, the sting of tears is a common human experience.

As a mother tenderly wipes the face of her hurting child, she knows tears will come again. The joy we experience in this world is only ever temporary. The joy of friendship, of love, of laughter or deep connection will eventually give way to the pain of saying goodbye. Joy is followed by sorrow. Smiles give way to tears. This is the inevitable reality of a world where everything dies.

But Isaiah holds out a stunning promise of what God will one day achieve:

> *The* Lord *Almighty … will swallow up death for ever. The Sovereign* Lord *will wipe away the tears from all faces. (Isaiah 25:6, 8)*

The image of God stooping down to his crying children and tenderly wiping away our tears is surely one of the most remarkable and intimate portraits of our beautiful Father in heaven. He is not a weak God who is sad but cannot help (he will swallow up death for ever). Neither is he a powerful God who is oblivious to our pain and sorrow (he wipes our tears away). On that day we will say goodbye to goodbyes.

Isaiah must have longed for that day but he didn't see it during his lifetime. Death still stalked and the tears still flowed. And we haven't seen it either.

But we have seen Jesus. He is the Sovereign Lord come in person—the tear-wiping God come close to his people. Jesus has walked our road. He was not embarrassed by human tears. He did not ignore human tears. Instead, he showed us there was hope.

While Jesus was once out walking with his disciples, he met a funeral procession. The circumstances of this occasion could hardly have been more tragic: a widow, who had already experienced the pain of losing her husband, has now been confronted with the death of her only son. Death has stripped this woman of everything precious. She is plunged into the darkest of nights. Her tears are flowing.

When Jesus sees her, he is deeply moved by the horrific reality of death. But then he says something remarkable, "Don't cry" (Luke 7:13). Seriously? What else is she supposed to do?

Yes, seriously. This was no awkward and meaningless platitude—it was a heart-stopping glimpse of the eternal hope of the gospel. Jesus demonstrated that he had both the compassion and the power to deal with her tears. He reversed death, raised the boy to life and gave him back to his mother. Sorrow to joy, death to life, the pain of goodbye to the warm hug of welcome.

Human tears are a liquid reminder of the deep pain that human sin has brought to this world. Therefore, the only possible way to deal with human tears is to deal with human sin.

And so, we find ourselves back again at the cross of Jesus. In that heart-wrenching moment, Jesus carried all our sin and our sorrow. He was overwhelmed. He experienced it. He paid for it. He defeated it. Then he rose again to a life of eternal joy with no more tears.

We still cry. We still wait. We still grieve. But our tears will no longer have the final word. When Jesus returns, he will wipe all your tears away. It will be the most precious thing to feel his nail-pierced hands on your face, reversing all the pain and bringing release from all the sorrow.

He does not ignore our tears nor play down our tears as if they don't matter. He doesn't tell us to pull ourselves together. He walks with us in our pain and then one day he will wipe it all away.

Jesus is wonderful because he is the only one who has the power to wipe our tears away for ever.

Knowing Jesus enables us to cry with hope. How does it help you today to know that your tears are important but temporary?

49

The Way Home

My soul yearns, even faints, for the courts of the Lord.

Psalm 84:2

The psalmist is homesick. He is in a far-off place and longs to be home. But he isn't craving a favourite armchair or a familiar pillow. He is dreaming of something much bigger. He longs to be back in the temple; he longs to be at home with God.

The vivid poetry of Psalm 84 is dripping with emotion and desire. The temple is "lovely" to him (v 1). He envies the simple little sparrow who has "found a home" near the altar (v 3). He longs to be among the worshippers who are "ever praising" God (v 4). In his mind, he pictures the journey back. He dreams of the "pilgrimage" (v 5). Even though the journey will lead through valleys, he knows there is blessing along the way (v 6). And all of it builds to the incredible moment when he might once again appear "before God in Zion" (v 7).

The temple was given by God to be the place of greatest delight and desire for his people. It was a place to daydream about, to sing about, and to set the heart upon. The temple was God's home—he came to live among his people. But although the temple was amazing, there was an even deeper dynamic going on.

The temple was designed to evoke memories of a much older home, reaching right back to the beginning of time and echoing the garden home that God created in Eden. It was in the garden that God and his people could dwell together in perfect relationship. No shame. No distance. No longing. It was the home we were created for.

But human sin ruined all of that. Our ancestors were banished from Eden. They were sent out to live in a hostile world. They were exiled to live away from home.

This is why the temple was such a precious gift—it held out the tantalising possibility of a glorious return home to Eden. No wonder the psalmist longed to be there. But, once again, God's people sinned against him and were driven into exile. The temple was broken down and the dream began to fade away. Was there any way home? It all seemed a distant memory.

If we can feel that heartache, it makes these words of Jesus all the more wonderful:

> *My Father's house has many rooms; if that were not so, would I have told you that I am going there to prepare a place for you? (John 14:2)*

When Jesus speaks of his Father's house, he is linking back to the imagery of the garden and the temple. The intimacy that was lost in Eden, and glimpsed in the temple, is about to be fulfilled in him. It won't be a temporary, limited, earthly building. Jesus is speaking of the eternal, solid hope of a garden-city, where God will perfectly dwell with his people for ever.

This is huge. We aren't supposed to picture a floaty mansion in a far-off place. Jesus' preparation doesn't involve rushing around getting things ready for our arrival. He isn't cleaning the rooms and putting out some flowers. No—the problem in Eden and the problem with the temple was that humanity messed it up. He prepares the way home by sorting out our hearts.

The road home for Jesus goes via the cross. He must go to the place of death in order to open the way. Jesus provides atonement for the very sin that would keep us away. As his hands and feet were nailed to that cross, he was preparing a place for us in God's eternal home.

And if he has prepared the way for us, do you think that he will then fail to bring us home? Of course not. When his disciple Thomas asks a clarification question about the precise way to this home, Jesus spells it out: "I am the way" (John 14:6). Jesus is the way home.

There is an eternal home that is worth longing for, daydreaming about and setting our hearts on. The promise of Eden and the hope of the temple will be completed in the new creation. The tragedy is that we often divert those longings towards other things. We seek out anything that will satisfy our desire for belonging and give us a sense of home. But nothing will ever fully be able to scratch that itch—the yearning runs too deep.

This is because we were created to be at home with God. And Jesus will bring you home.

Jesus is wonderful because he is the way home.

Read Psalm 84 and ask God to grow your longing to be in his eternal home.

50

The Morning Star

I am the Root and the Offspring of David,
and the bright Morning Star.

Revelation 22:16

Jesus tells his suffering church that he is the bright Morning Star. It is the final description of Jesus in the Bible, and it could not be a more inspiring place to end. It will correct our thinking and set our perspective straight. We so often get things the wrong way round.

Try this: do you think that night follows day or that day follows night? Seriously, it is far more significant than you might first imagine.

A modern Western mindset would say that there is day and then night comes. It is the way we talk. It is the way we run our lives. Monday morning, Monday afternoon, Monday evening. But in Bible thinking it is the other way round. You can feel it in the very rhythm of creation.

"There was evening, and there was morning—the first day" (Genesis 1:5). Evening then morning. Night then day. Darkness then light. The Jewish calendar reflected this understanding—Sabbath began at sundown on the Friday.

Could it be that the day-then-night view of the world feels more natural in a culture that is ultimately pessimistic about the future. Our time on earth is short. We have a brief daytime of life. We need to do all that we can; we enjoy life, we do good and we make the most of it before the sun sets on our lives and we are plunged into darkness. This also mirrors the narrative we are constantly told about our planet. It is a beautiful place but eventually darkness will win, our world will be destroyed, and night will come. At the end of the day, the night triumphs.

But a night-then-day perspective sparkles with a bright optimism for the future. It enables us to live with a realistic expectation of this present age and to look ahead to the bright light of day.

The great back and forth battle between day and night will not continue for ever. It will eventually end with an unequivocal victory for the day. This is beautifully captured in this simple statement about the future God has prepared for us: "There will be no more night" (Revelation 22:5). The day wins!

All the darkness will be vanquished from the land—all the fear, the sorrow, the shame, the shadows, the enemies. The night will be over, and we will enjoy this eternal day with Jesus for ever. The future for our world is not dark extinction but bright transformation. Can you imagine it? This world but without any darkness of night?

It sounds great, but we aren't there yet. Sometimes it feels like the night will never end. This is why we need to know that Jesus is the Morning Star.

Imagine a soldier posted to stand duty through the watches of the night. The cloak of darkness threatens; the enemy seems to be hiding in every shadow. Fear and anxiety grip his heart as the minutes crawl past. But then, right before dawn, piercing the darkness of the night appears a bright shining star—a defiant herald proclaiming to the soldier that the night is nearly over and the day is about to come. When the morning star appears, hope surges and anticipation rises. We are nearly there. The day is coming soon.

Jesus is that bright Morning Star who has already risen in the sky. The darkness surrounds us, but we see him shining. The shadows threaten us but we see him as victorious. Death hunts us, but we see him as the Living One (Revelation 1:18). The night continues but the Morning Star has appeared. That must mean that very, very soon, the day will be here.

The final words of Jesus in the whole Bible proclaim this hope: "Yes, I am coming soon" (Revelation 22:20). Hold on dear friends. Let hope surge in your hearts. The night will pass, Jesus is shining, and the day is nearly here. So we respond with hearts of faith, "Amen. Come, Lord Jesus."

Jesus is wonderful because he is the bright Morning Star that proclaims to the world that the night is nearly over and the day *will* win!

How will you continue to trust in the bright Morning Star and increasingly delight in Jesus?

BIBLICAL | RELEVANT | ACCESSIBLE

At The Good Book Company we are dedicated to helping Christians and local churches grow. We believe that God's growth process always starts with hearing clearly what he has said to us through his timeless and flawless word—the Bible.

Ever since we opened our doors in 1991, we have been striving to produce resources that are biblical, relevant, and accessible. By God's grace, we have grown to become an international publisher, encouraging ordinary Christians of every age and stage and every background and denomination to live for Christ day by day and equipping churches to grow in their knowledge of God, their love for one another, and the effectiveness of their outreach.

Call one of our friendly team for a discussion of your needs or visit one of our local websites for more information on the resources and services we provide.

Your friends at The Good Book Company